D0167321

Jamie Malanowski,

Lisa Birnbach, and

Kurt Andersen

A FIRESIDE BOOK

Published by Simon & Schuster

New York   London   Toronto   Sydney   Tokyo   Singapore

Loose Lips

Real Words
Real People
Real Funny

FIRESIDE
Rockefeller Center
1230 Avenue of the Americas
New York, NY 10020

FIRESIDE and colophon are registered trademarks
of Simon & Schuster Inc.

Designed by Hyun Joo Kim

Manufactured in the United States of America

1   3   5   7   9   10   8   6   4   2

Library of Congress Cataloging-in-Publication Data

Malanowski, Jamie.
Loose lips : real words   real people   real funny / by Jamie
Malanowski, Lisa Birnbach, and Kurt Andersen.
          p.   cm.
1. Celebrities—Quotations.   I. Birnbach, Lisa.   II. Andersen, Kurt.
                    III. Title.
          PN6084.C44M35   1995
     081—dc20   95-21888
                    CIP

ISBN 0-684-80340-2

ACKNOWLEDGMENTS

The authors wish to thank the following people:
Martin Charnin. Marilyn Abraham. Becky Cabaza.
Jimmy Biberi. Scott Bryant. Sara Pratter. Keith Primi.
Ingrid Rockefeller. Luke Toma. Mark Smaltz. Ira
Hawkins. Sean Altman. John Brodie. Colin Callender.
John Connolly. Lynda Edwards. Leon Friedman. Fred
Goodman. Chris Gore. Flo Grace. Graydon Carter.
Joanne Gruber. Bruce Handy. David Hochman. Mark
Lasswell. Patricia Marx. Jeff Ressner. Chip Rowe. Brad
Ruskin. Louis Theroux. Steve and Nancy McGraw. Pe-
ter Martin. Jim and Judy Hart. Deborah Slater. Heather
Holst. James Geppner. George Sheanshang. David Kor-
zenik. Dick Ticktin. Eric Rayman. Roger Gindi. Peter
Cromarty. Jon Wilner. Robert Best. Erv Raible. Martin
Kaufman. Caroline Hirsch. Jaye Lee. Ken Foy. Ken
Billington. Keith Levinson. Richard Mauro. Stu Smiley.
Jon Rubin. Bridget Potter. Jack Lechner. Wally Rubin.
Tom Manning. Charlie Sturkin. Ron Livian. Diana
Chapin. Mike Egan. Steven Haft. Ginny Jackson. Anne
Kreamer.

We know who you are, and we know what you did.

CONTENTS

INTRODUCTION

IN THE VERY FIRST ISSUE OF SPY MAGAZINE nine years ago, we established a feature called "The Fine Print." This was the main place in the magazine for publishing any kind of intriguing raw data. We required simply that the information be both interesting and none of our business. We published digests of ghastly coroners' findings, voting records of TV anchorpeople, details of litigation between the sorts of people who buy art for Sylvester Stallone and Sylvester Stallone—and transcripts of conversations between people who would prefer that their conversations remain unpublicized, if not private.

We developed a special taste for this last sort of artifact. We aren't sure why. Maybe we were, in our attenuated way, carrying on the work of Marcel Duchamp and sixties Pop, selecting bits of improbable prefab reality and declaring those bits worthy of intense but not altogether serious scrutiny. Maybe it was the end of the cold war and the decline of organized crime. (With hardly any communists or gangsters to eavesdrop on, Marion Barry and rowdy baseball players became the next best thing, surrogate threats-to-our-way-of-life, targets lite.) Maybe it was an ultimate extension of the death of fiction: in the hyperliteralist, celebrocentric *age of* People *and* Vanity Fair, *C-Span and Court TV, only absolutely documentary truth would satisfy. Or maybe we were just badly brought up.*

In any event, during our final months together at Spy *in late 1992, the British tabloids published excerpts of a somewhat mysteriously recorded telephone conversation between Prince Charles and his mistress. One morning, two of us put on the plummiest English accents we could muster and read the conversation aloud. It made us laugh, which led us to imagine that an entertaining night of theater, overseen by an authentic director (instead of Jamie) and featuring professional actors (instead of Kurt and Lisa), could be confected from such material.*

And so it was. A year later we persuaded the veteran stage director Martin Charnin that our transcript theater was a project worth squandering his time and considerable reputation on, and he in turn persuaded a half-dozen actors (James Biberi, Sara Prater, Luke Toma, Keith Primi, Ingrid Rockefeller, and Scott Bryant) to jeopardize their nascent careers and join us. Then investors signed on, then cable TV executives, then book editors, and now you've been sucked in.

It was a joyride that got out of hand.

Because this enterprise is original in its profound unoriginality (court transcripts have been turned into serious agitprop theater before, but never, as far as we know, played for kicks) and vaguely illicit, we have not been rigid about criteria. Some of the material has been unearthed from straightforward public documents (congressional testimony, legal depositions, and the like), but much of it is from shadowier sources—wire-

taps, scanners, studio outtakes, telephone answering machines, samizdat transcriptions of various kinds. As far as we can determine, everything here is accurately rendered, although we've edited for clarity and brevity. And no animals have been harmed in the making of this production.

Looking over the transcripts now, in aggregate, we noticed that a slight majority of the material concerns, in some measure, sex. (This does not include, however, the conversation between Los Angeles Dodgers manager Tommy Lasorda and two of his players, even though Lasorda uses some permutation of the word "fuck" twenty-two times.)

Sometimes the conversations are interesting because they are so private—which usually means they satisfyingly confirm our suspicions of how people talk when ordinary citizens aren't around (one thinks of Tommy Lasorda, page 19), but it can also mean the opposite (one thinks of the prissy mafiosi on page 191). And other times the conversations are interesting because they are—with their bald evasions, their hubris, their who's-on-first misunderstandings—so shockingly public, pieces of legal or legislative ritual whose implicit comedy or weirdness is revealed merely by plucking the conversations out of their familiar contexts to be looked at freshly, attentively, cruelly.

For those taking notes, it turns out that each of the conversationalists we've collected tends to fall into one of seven categories.

There are political Washingtonians: presidents (Ronald Reagan, Gerald Ford, Bill Clinton), presidential wannabes (Robert Dole), presidential hangers-on

(Gennifer Flowers), congressional aides, and mayors who have served prison time for crack cocaine possession.

Then there are foreign dignitaries having intimate conversations with their chums: the Prince of Wales (with Camilla Parker Bowles), the Princess of Wales (with James Gilbey), Anwar Sadat (with Gerald Ford), Saddam Hussein (with Senator Alan Simpson).

High-strung movie directors constitute a category all their own: Orson Welles, Jerry Lewis, Francis Coppola, Woody Allen, and Spike Lee. So do middle-aged, lower-middle-brow TV stars: Roseanne, Tom Snyder, Ted Danson, Casey Kasem; and so do classic rockers: John Lennon, Bruce Springsteen.

There are Litigants, Misc.—various little-known criminals and various little-known lawyers. Finally, there are leaders of men (various tobacco executives and the aforementioned Tommy Lasorda).

Sometimes these scenes are funny. Sometimes they are alarming. And lots of times they are both.

"I May Be Wrong, but That's My Goddamn Job"

IT'S ONE OF BASEBALL'S OLDEST QUESTIONS: Exactly what do managers say to pitchers when they go out to the mound during a game? Well, here's the answer. During the 1977 World Series, when the Los Angeles Dodgers were facing the New York Yankees, a television executive thought it would be a good idea to put a microphone on Tommy Lasorda, the manager of the Dodgers. We pick up the action in Game 4. It's the second inning. The Yanks are ahead one to nothing, they're leading the series two games to one, and they've got men on second and third, with none out. The Dodger pitcher, Doug Rau, is about to go into his windup—wait, here comes Lasorda.

DOUG RAU
Come on, Tommy, let me stay in the game.

TOMMY LASORDA
Fuck, no. You can't get the fucking left-handers out, for Christ all-fucking-mighty.

RAU
I feel good, Tommy.

LASORDA
I don't give a shit you feel good. There's four motherfucking hits up there.

RAU
> They're all fucking hits the opposite way.

LASORDA
> I don't give a fuck.

RAU
> There's a left-handed hitter coming up. I can strike this motherfucker out.

LASORDA
> I don't give a shit, Dougie.

RAU
> I think you're wrong.

LASORDA
> Well, I may be wrong, but that's my goddamn job.

RAU
> I ain't fucking hurting.

LASORDA
> I'll make the fucking decisions here, okay? I'll make the fucking decisions.

RAU
> You let three runs get up there on the fucking board yesterday!

LASORDA
> *I don't give a fuck!*

RAU
　Hey, Tommy, I—

LASORDA
　Don't give me any shit, goddammit! I'll make the fucking decisions. Keep your fucking mouth shut, I told ya.

　One of the infielders comes to the mound to calm Lasorda down.

INFIELDER
　Hey, guys, why don't you get back off the mound? You want to talk about it, talk about it inside.

LASORDA
　You talk about it inside my fucking office.

INFIELDER
　I'm just saying talk about it inside. This is not the place to keep talking about it, okay? That's all I'm trying to say. I'm just trying to avoid a fucking scene out here, okay?

LASORDA
　Right. Fucking great for you to be standing out here talking to me like that.

RAU
　I wouldn't say anything if I didn't feel good.

LASORDA
　And I don't give a shit, Doug. I'm the fucking manager of the fucking team. I got to make the fucking de-

cisions, and I'll make them to the best of my ability. It may be the fucking wrong decision, but I'll make it. Don't worry about it, I'll make the fucking decision. I can't fuck around. We're down two games to one. If it was yesterday, that's a different story.

RAU

But there's a left-hander coming up.

LASORDA

I don't give a shit! You had three left-handed hitters, they all got hits on you. Whoever that is, Jackson, and that fucking other guy. That guy that just hit the ball off you—he was a left-hander, wasn't he? You didn't get him out.

RAU

But I jammed him!

LASORDA

I don't give a shit if you jammed him or not, you didn't get him out. I can't leave you out there in a fucking game like this—I got a fucking job to do. Understand? I got a fucking job to do!

Rau left the mound, but for the record, the Yanks still won the game—and the fucking series.

"A Little Dog Named Snuckles"

EVERYBODY IS ENTITLED TO LOSE HIS OR her temper from time to time. The point is not to lose it in front of an open microphone. Casey Kasem, the host of the nationally syndicated countdown program, American Top Forty, *apparently just forgot.*

CASEY KASEM
Now it's time for our long-distance dedication, and this one's about kids, and pets, and a situation that we can all understand, whether we have kids, or pets, or neither. It's from a man in Cincinnati, Ohio, and here's what he writes.

"Dear Casey, This may seem to be a strange dedication request, but I'm quite sincere, and it'll mean a lot if you play it. Recently, there was a death in our family. He was a little dog named Snuckles. He was most certainly a part of—"

Let's start again, from comin' out of the record.

Play the record, okay? *Please.* See, when you come out of those uptempo goddamn numbers, man, it's impossible to make those transitions, and then you gotta go into somebody *dying.*

You know, they do this to me all the time, I don't know what the hell they do it for, but goddammit, if we can't come out of a slow record, I don't understand— Is Don on the phone? *Okay.* I want a goddamn concerted effort to come out of a record that isn't a fucking uptempo record every time I do a goddamn *death* dedication. Now make it—and I also want to know what happened to the pictures I was supposed to see this week! This is a—this is the last goddamn time—I want somebody to use his fuckin' brain to not come out of a goddamn record that is, uh, that's uptempo, and I gotta talk about a fuckin' *dog* dying.

Also from the Casey collection is the following outtake:

Here's the first Top Forty hit for the Irish band from Dublin who call themselves U2. That's the letter U and the numeral 2. The four-man band features Adam Clayton on bass, Larry Mullen on drums, Dale Evans, nicknamed "The Edge," on. . . . This is bullshit, nobody cares. These guys are from England, and who gives a shit? It's a lot of wasted names that don't mean diddlyshit!

"There's Just Too Much Directing Going On Around Here"

NOT LONG BEFORE HE DIED, ORSON WELLES, the brilliant actor and director who gave us The Magnificent Ambersons, The War of the Worlds, *and* Citizen Kane, *found himself in a recording studio in London, doing voice-overs for a series of commercials for British frozen food. We join the great Welles, and his directors, in progress.*

ORSON WELLES
"We know a remote farm in Lincolnshire where Mrs. Buckley lives. Every July, peas grow there." Do you really mean that?

DIRECTOR I
Yeah. See, in other words, I-I-I'd start a half a second later—

WELLES
Don't you think you really want to say "July" over the snow? Isn't that the fun of it?

DIRECTOR I
It's—it's— If you could almost make it when that shot disappears, it'd make my life—

WELLES
I think it's so nice that you see a snow-covered field

and say, "Every July, peas grow there." See? "We know a remote farm in Lincolnshire, where Mrs. Buckley lives. In July, peas grow there."

DIRECTOR II
Could you emphasize a bit "In"? "*In* July"?

WELLES
Why? That doesn't make any sense. Sorry.

DIRECTOR II
Um, well—

WELLES
There's no known way of saying an English sentence in which you begin a sentence with "in" and emphasize it. Get me a jury and show me how you can say "*In* July" and I'll go down on you. That's just idiotic, if you'll forgive my saying so. That's just stupid. "*In* July." I'd love to know how to emphasize "*In*" in "*In* July." Impossible! Meaningless! Unwelcoming!

DIRECTOR I
I think all he was thinking about was that he didn't want to—

WELLES
He isn't thinking.

DIRECTOR II
Orson, can we do just one last thing?

WELLES
Yeah.

DIRECTOR I
It was my fault. I-I-I said, "In July." If you could leave it "Every July"—

WELLES
You didn't say it; he said it. Your *friend*. You don't really mean "Every July"; it's "In July." There's just too much directing going on around here. And now I have no more time. You don't know what I'm up against.

DIRECTOR I
Let's move on.

WELLES
Here, under protest, is beefburgers. "We know a little place in the American Far West where Charlie Briggs chops up the finest prairie-fed beef, and tastes—" This is a lot of *shit,* you know that.

DIRECTOR II
Yeah.

WELLES
You want one more?

DIRECTOR I
You missed the first beef, actually, completely. You were emphasizing "prairie-fed"—

WELLES
But you can't emphasize "beef"! That's like his wanting me to emphasize *"In"* in *"In* July." Come on, you're

losing your heads! I wouldn't direct any living actor like this in Shakespeare! The way you do this, it's impossible—

DIRECTOR II
   Orson, you did six last year, and they were far and away the best—

WELLES
   The right reading for this is the one I'm giving you. I spend *twenty* times more for you people than any other commercial I've ever made. You're such *pests!* Now what is it you want? In the depths of your ignorance, what is it you want?

   Welles starts rumbling out of the studio.

DIRECTOR II
   That was absolutely fine, whatever way it was.

"I Got a Fucking Master of Fine Arts"

ON MARCH 1, 1992, THE NEW YORK TIMES *published an article about Spike Lee and a course on contemporary African American cinema he was teaching at Harvard. The article contained the following sentence: "Some students and faculty members have questioned Mr. Lee's qualifications to teach because he does not have a college degree." Before long, "Professor Spike," as he had encouraged his students to call him, left the following message on the answering machine of a reporter at the* Times's *culture desk.*

SPIKE LEE
This is Spike Lee. How you doing? Look, how in the hell are you going to write some bullshit that I don't have a fucking college degree? I got a fucking master's from NYU and an undergraduate degree from Morehouse College. How's the fucking *New York Times* gonna write some bullshit that I don't have a fucking college degree? You know, you motherfuckers ought to do some fucking research or whatever you call that shit before you write some fucking bullshit, all right? I got a fucking master of fine arts from fucking NYU. I want a motherfucking retraction. All right, motherfucker?

A correction appeared before the week was out.

"Gossip Can Finish Me Off"

MOVIEMAKING, AS THEY SAY, IS A RELATION-
*ship business, and its creative community, as they call
it, consists of people like famously warm, hearty, passionate Francis Coppola, for example. The following
transcript is from a conversation Coppola had (and
that his wife tape-recorded) on the set of his epic film*
Apocalypse Now *in the Philippines. Coppola—whose
project is in debt and desperately behind schedule, who
has already seen millions of dollars' worth of sets de-
stroyed by a hurricane, who has to cope with Marlon
Brando—has just received a bit of shocking news: his
leading man, Martin Sheen, has suffered a heart attack.
In this conversation, he is making it clear to an associate that he doesn't want that news to get out.*

FRANCIS COPPOLA

Dave Salvin let Melissa tell Barry Hirsch that Marty
had a heart attack. What the *fuck* is that? What the
fuck *is* that? Do you know it's going to be all over Hollywood in a half an hour? If Marty is so seriously
stricken, then, that he must go back, then of course he
will go back and we'll eat it. But when I talked to
the doctor, they didn't know. Marty's a young man; he
probably would be able to be up and about in three
weeks. I said, "Could he do nonstrenuous work, such
as close-ups, or sitting and acting?" He said, "Possibly

yes." That's all I need to hear from the doctor. So what's going on in the fucking trades is fucking gossip. *Gossip.* That gossip can finish me off. Because if UA hears that it's eight weeks, UA—with a $27 million negative—is going to force me to complete it with what I've got. And I don't have the movie yet.

ASSOCIATE
  Right.

COPPOLA
  All right, then you understand exactly.

ASSOCIATE
  Yes.

COPPOLA
  If Marty dies . . . I want to hear everything is okay until I say, "Marty is dead." You got it?

ASSOCIATE
  Right.

"Just Answer It Yes or No"

IN 1991, TWO MEN WHO HAD WORKED AS roadies for Bruce Springsteen sued him, claiming he had promised to pay them more than they had actually received. (What? Proximity to people more charismatic and talented than you isn't enough anymore?) The suit would eventually get settled out of court, but before that could happen, the Boss, just like defendants who do not have colorful nicknames, had to give a deposition and respond to questions from the plaintiffs' attorney.

LAWYER

A couple rules about traffic, okay? We all have ways of answering questions with a "yup" or a "uh-huh" or a "um-hmm." As I'm sure you realize, it's difficult for the court stenographer to take that down and then put it in a transcript so that someone else can read it and then understand that when you were saying "uh-huh" or "um-hmm" you meant yes or no. So I may from time to time just stop you and say, "Just answer it yes or no." Okay? Do you understand?

BRUCE SPRINGSTEEN

Um-hmmm.

"Was It More Than Fifty?"

THERE ARE TENS OF THOUSANDS OF LAWYERS in New York City. Among the more creative is a litigator named Barry Agulnick. Back in 1989, a police officer who was assigned to patrol the subways was accused of making false arrests. As part of his defense, his attorney, the zealous Mr. Agulnick, tested out a unique legal strategy. He tried to suggest that even if those people who'd been falsely arrested weren't, in fact, committing the crimes they were being arrested for at the time of their arrests, well, they might have committed those offenses at some other time.

Anyway, here's Mr. Agulnick, in court, cross-examining a young man who had been accused of lewdly rubbing himself against a woman on the subway.

BARRY AGULNICK
Now, sir, I ask you to think back to that subway ride, and to the ten-minute period you were on that train. During that ride, did you have an erection?

MAN
No, I did not.

AGULNICK
Are you sure of that?

MAN
  I'm sure.

AGULNICK
  Do you remember being asked this question in March of 1987?

MAN
  Yes.

AGULNICK
  And do you remember that at that time, your answer was "I don't recall having one"?

MAN
  Well, I didn't.

AGULNICK
  Did you give that answer under oath?

MAN
  Yes, I did.

AGULNICK
  That you didn't *recall* having one.

MAN
  Right.

AGULNICK
  And now you're telling us you're *certain* that you didn't have one.

MAN
Absolutely, I did not.

AGULNICK
Have you ever had an erection?

MAN
Oh, sure.

AGULNICK
On the train?

MAN
No—on the train, yes, maybe I had, yes. I wouldn't say I didn't have one anytime on the train. Not that day.

AGULNICK
Ever while you were standing on the train?

MAN
No!

AGULNICK
Did you ever have an erection while you were standing next to an attractive female on the train?

MAN
No!

AGULNICK
On how many occasions have you had erections on the train?

MAN
I can't answer that question.

AGULNICK
Is it too numerous to mention?

MAN
I never counted them if I did have them.

AGULNICK
Was it more than fifty?

MAN
I don't know.

AGULNICK
When you had an erection on the train, was it due to your looking at someone?

MAN
Not necessarily.

AGULNICK
You mean this is just something that happens on the train?

MAN
Doesn't have to be on the train.

AGULNICK
But we're talking about the train. And you've said you had numerous times when you've had erections on the train.

MAN
You said numerous times.

AGULNICK
Well, how many times was it, sir?

MAN
I really don't know.

AGULNICK
Well, those times that you've had erections on the train, were any of those erections caused by your rubbing against the anatomy of a female?

MAN
No.

AGULNICK
You sure of that?

MAN
Positive.

AGULNICK
What caused those erections on the train?

MAN
The body.

AGULNICK
Your body?

MAN
The normal procedure of a body.

AGULNICK
Do you think about certain things on a train that cause the erection?

MAN
No.

AGULNICK
Are you telling us that it's your testimony that you can't tell us the circumstances under which you get erections on the train? Is that correct?

MAN
Correct.

AGULNICK
I have no further questions for this witness.

The police officer was convicted of making false arrests.

"You Are Going to Be Dating Me"

AMONG THE MORE CAPTIVATING CIRCUSES staged by our government in recent years was the Clarence Thomas hearings. You'll recall that in October 1991, Anita Hill accused Judge Thomas of sexually harassing her, first when she was his assistant at the Department of Education, and then again when she had a similar post and he served as chairman of the Equal Employment Opportunity Commission. Her testimony was compelling. You'll recall that Thomas then rebutted her. His testimony—an absolute denial—was compelling too. With two credible witnesses, you have to ask yourself: What might have tipped the balance? Suppose another woman who had a similar experience was willing to come forward.

As it turned out, there was such a woman. Her name was Angela Wright, a newspaperwoman from Charlotte who had previously worked for Thomas as the head of the PR department at the EEOC. Three days before Hill gave her testimony on national television, Wright was interviewed over the telephone by members of the Senate Judiciary Committee staff.

CYNTHIA HOGAN
   Hi, Angela. This is Cynthia Hogan from the Senate

Judiciary Committee. I'm sorry we're calling you a little bit later than we had anticipated, but it took us a little bit of time to get ourselves together this morning. I told you last night that someone from Senator Thurmond's staff would be here, and that I would be here. Actually, there are two people here from Senator Biden's office, myself and Harriet Grant, and two people here from Senator Thurmond's office, as well as four other lawyers, who work for other senators. But only two people are going to ask you questions, and that is me and Terry Wooten, who works for Senator Thurmond. Is that all right?

ANGELA WRIGHT
   Yes.

HOGAN
   Ms. Wright, as I understand it, you know Clarence Thomas, is that correct?

WRIGHT
   That is correct.

HOGAN
   It's also my understanding that you worked with Clarence Thomas at the EEOC, is that correct?

WRIGHT
   That is correct.

HOGAN
   And your title was what?

WRIGHT
Director of Public Affairs.

HOGAN
And did you report to Clarence Thomas?

WRIGHT
Yes, I did.

HOGAN
Did you consider your relationship with Clarence Thomas at this time to be strictly professional?

WRIGHT
I considered Clarence Thomas at the time to be— well, I guess you could say it was strictly professional, in that there was no other contact between me and Clarence Thomas outside of professional activities.

HOGAN
Can you tell me—were there comments that he made to you that maybe you considered inappropriate?

WRIGHT
Yes. I can tell you that during the course of the year that I worked for Clarence Thomas, there were several comments that he made. Clarence Thomas did consistently pressure me to date him. At one point, Clarence Thomas made comments about my anatomy. Clarence Thomas made comments about women's anatomy quite often. At one point, Clarence Thomas came by my

apartment at night, unannounced and uninvited, and talked in general terms about the prospect of my dating him.

HOGAN
Do you remember the first comment or conduct Clarence Thomas engaged in that you considered inappropriate?

WRIGHT
No, I do not. I cannot sit here and tell you I remember dates. What I can tell you is that this is a general course of action, this is an attitude and these are comments that Clarence Thomas has generally tended to make.

HOGAN
Okay. You mentioned that generally he pressured you to date him.

WRIGHT
Yes.

HOGAN
Was there anything that occurred along those lines prior to the time he came to your apartment?

WRIGHT
Yes.

HOGAN
Can you tell us about that?

WRIGHT
Let me be specific here. We are not talking about, you know, traumatic single events here. We're talking about a general mode of operating. I can remember specifically one evening when the comment about dating came up. The EEOC was having a retirement party for my predecessor, Al Sweeney. And we were sitting at the banquet table while the speakers were going through their speeches, and Clarence Thomas was sitting right next to me, and at one point he turned around and said, "You look good, and you are going to be dating me, too." That was not, like, the only time he said something of that nature.

HOGAN
Was anyone else sitting there with you?

WRIGHT
Well, there were several people at the banquet table.

HOGAN
Do you know whether any of them heard this comment?

WRIGHT
I seriously doubt any of them heard it. He was sitting right next to me, and this wasn't something he was shouting. He was practically whispering, because there was a program going on.

HOGAN
Was there any further discussion of what he said?

WRIGHT
  No.

HOGAN
  Did you respond in any way?

WRIGHT
  No, I never did.

HOGAN
  Do you remember any other occasions when he pressured you to date him?

WRIGHT
  No, I do not. I can't give you dates and times.

HOGAN
  Why don't you tell us what you remember in general?

WRIGHT
  In general, given the opportunity, Clarence Thomas is the type of person—well, let me back up a minute. In general, given the opportunity, Clarence Thomas would say to me, "You need to be dating me, I think I'm going to date you, you're one of the finest women I have on my staff, we're going to be going out eventually."

HOGAN
  What do you mean, given the opportunity?

WRIGHT
  Given the opportunity—you know, if there was no

one else around or we were close enough that he could turn around and whisper something of that nature.

HOGAN

You mentioned this occurred once at your apartment. Can you tell me a little bit more about that?

WRIGHT

He came to my apartment, I opened the door, I offered him a beer, we sat at a counter separating the kitchen and the living room, and talked in general about general things, and, you know, the conversation would turn to his desire to date me. And I would adeptly turn it to another topic.

HOGAN

And he arrived uninvited?

WRIGHT

Yes, that is correct.

HOGAN

Did he say why he had come to your apartment?

WRIGHT

Not that I can recall. My recollection was that he was in the neighborhood or something, but I can't actually recall any specific things about the conversation. You know, I wish I could, but it's not the kind of thing I was taking notes about.

HOGAN

No, I can certainly understand that. I'm just asking for specific recollections if you have them.

WRIGHT

I can specifically recall being at a seminar—I can't recall which seminar, we had so many of them—when Clarence Thomas commented on the dress I was wearing and asked me what size my boobs were.

HOGAN

This was at an EEOC conference?

WRIGHT

An EEOC seminar, yes.

MR. TERRY WOOTEN

Can we go back to the time frame when you say Judge Thomas came to your apartment? I don't know that we got the time frame. Can you give us a specific date?

WRIGHT

Well, it was not in the summer. It was like it was cold, like the end of fall or early winter.

WOOTEN

The next thing you mentioned was this EEOC seminar. Do you have any recollection of when this occurred?

WRIGHT

No; we were to several seminars. My only recollection of it was that we were walking towards a meeting room and I was briefing him.

WOOTEN

Do you remember the subject of the seminar?

WRIGHT

The seminars generally were about the laws under which the EEOC operated. We held seminars to tell people, you know, this is what qualifies as age discrimination, this qualifies as sexual harassment . . .

HOGAN

Do you know whether anyone overheard the comment?

WRIGHT

No, I don't.

HOGAN

Did you tell anyone about it?

WRIGHT

No, I didn't. No, let me put it this way—I didn't walk away from that situation and say, you know, guess what Clarence Thomas just said.

HOGAN

Okay.

WRIGHT

But in the course of other conversations, particularly with women, about Clarence Thomas, yes, I have relayed that situation, along with all others.

HOGAN

Do you recall that any of those women had a particular reaction?

WRIGHT
I recall one. And I—I can almost quote her, as a matter of fact. "Well," she said, "he's a man, you know. He's always hitting on everybody."

HOGAN
I'm sorry, I didn't catch that.

WRIGHT
He's always hitting on everybody.

HOGAN
Can you tell me the circumstances under which you left the EEOC?

WRIGHT
Yes. Clarence Thomas fired me.

HOGAN
Can you describe the circumstances?

WRIGHT
Sure. I came into my office one day and there was a letter on my chair, and I read the letter, and it said: "Your services here are no longer needed." It was quite a surprise to me. I took the letter and went upstairs to his office, and I said to him, "What is this? Why are you firing me?" And he said, "Well, Angela, I've never been satisfied with your work." I said, "Why have you not told me this up to this point?"' And he said, "Well, I told you to fire all those folks down there,

and you haven't fired a soul." And I said, "Clarence, those are career employees; it's not like I can just go in and say, You're fired. It takes almost an act of Congress to get them removed."

He said, "Well, I just in general am not satisfied with your work." The day prior to that, we had a press conference. I don't remember what the issue was, but it was a very successful press conference. All the major media were there. And that morning, as we were talking, he had a folder in front of him with almost an inch of clippings in it. So I picked that up and said, "How can you say that, today of all days?" And he said, "I never needed you to get me publicity. I can always call the *Washington Post*."

And I said, "Okay, fine. This is your prerogative. You could tell me to go because you don't like the color of my shoes. But why did you decide to do this? If you wanted me to leave, all you had to do was go to your friends at the White House and get me another appointment. But your intent was to make me unemployed. Why is that? I have tried to be a loyal employee. I have tried to be your friend."

And he said, "Well, I have never cared anything about loyalty, and I don't care a whole lot about friendship." And I pushed the chair away from the table and said, "Well, I hope you will be a very happy, successful man, but I doubt it." And I walked out of his office.

HOGAN

Do you think your failure to respond to any of Judge Thomas's comments to you had anything to do with him firing you?

WRIGHT

You know, you are not the first person who has asked me that question. Several people at the EEOC asked me that.

HOGAN

Are there other specific comments that Judge Thomas made that you want to tell us about?

WRIGHT

Well—about the only thing I can tell you is that at one point in that conversation about why he was firing me, he said that he was real bothered by the fact that I did not wait for him outside his office after work. It was a statement I dismissed as just one of his statements.

HOGAN

So you didn't follow up or respond?

WRIGHT

I don't remember responding. You know, I wasn't a very happy person at that point.

HOGAN

Ms. Wright, do you know Anita Hill?

WRIGHT

I have never met Anita Hill, and I have never heard of Anita Hill before this week.

HOGAN

You are, I take it, aware of Professor Hill's allegations about Clarence Thomas?

WRIGHT

Yes, I am.

HOGAN

Do you feel that those allegations are in or out of character for Clarence Thomas, as you know him?

WRIGHT

I feel that the Clarence Thomas that I know is quite capable of doing just what Anita Hill alleges.

WOOTEN

Can you tell us just what your feelings were at the time you heard Clarence Thomas had been nominated to the Supreme Court?

WRIGHT

I never wavered in my feelings about that. I don't think Clarence Thomas is a good man, and I don't think he should be on the Supreme Court.

WOOTEN

But about why you came forward—is the thrust of your concern about Judge Thomas—is it the comments that he made to you, or is it your general belief that he should not be on the Supreme Court?

WRIGHT

The thrust of my concern at this point was to not watch a woman who I believe in my gut to be telling the truth about a man who I believe to be totally capable of doing what she said he did—the thrust of my concern was not to watch her become victimized, when I know of similar situations I had with Mr. Thomas.

Later, Cynthia Hogan told Angela Wright that she should be prepared to testify. At that point, Wright flew to Washington and waited for the committee to call her. Hogan also asked Wright if there was anyone who could corroborate her statements. Wright gave them the name of Rose Jourdain, who had worked with her at the EEOC. At that point, Jourdain was in the hospital undergoing surgery. By the time the Senate aides got on the phone and interviewed her, it was Sunday afternoon: Hill had spoken, Thomas had spoken, and the committee was working its way through the first of several panels of character witnesses. Here is what Jourdain had to say.

MARY DeOREO
Rose, this is Mary DeOreo from the Senate Judiciary Committee. Sitting in the room with me are representatives of Senator Biden's staff, Senator Heflin's staff, and Senator Leahy's staff, and there are also represenatives from the minority side. I understand that this interview is taking place while you are at the Washington Hospital Center, so we are going to try to stay on the point and not take too long. Now, when were you employed at the EEOC?

ROSE JOURDAIN
I believe it was November '83 to March '85. I think those are the correct dates.

DeOREO
  What was your position at the EEOC?

JOURDAIN
  I was a speechwriter for the chairman, Clarence Thomas.

DeOREO
  At that time, did you know Anita Hill?

JOURDAIN
  No, I never met her.

DeOREO
  During the course of your working as a speechwriter for Judge Thomas, did you meet with him personally?

JOURDAIN
  Yes, and frequently.

DeOREO
  Did you experience any sort of harassment from Judge Thomas?

JOURDAIN
  I personally? None.

DeOREO
  Do you know Angela Wright?

JOURDAIN
  Yes, I do. She was the head of the public relations department at the EEOC.

DeOREO
   Did Ms. Wright ever discuss with you any concerns or problems she was having in her encounters with Judge Thomas?

JOURDAIN
   Yes, she did.

DeOREO
   Can you give me some specific details as to what Ms. Wright told you?

JOURDAIN
   When Ms. Wright first came in, she was very enthusiastic about her job. She was very happy to be there. As time went on, she became increasingly—she confided to me increasingly that she was a little uneasy, and that she grew more uneasy with the chairman, because of comments she told me that he was making concerning her figure, her body, her breasts, her legs, how she looked in certain suits and dresses.

DeOREO
   Did she recount any specific experience?

JOURDAIN
   Well, for example, she told me he had come to her home one night unannounced, and she told everyone—for example, one time she came to my office in tears, and she had bought a new suit that I thought was quite attractive, but it was just a regular suit for a person to wear to work, a woman to wear to work—and he evidently had had quite a bit of comment to

make about it, and how sexy she looked in it and that kind of thing, and it unnerved her a great deal.

She became increasingly nervous about being in his presence alone. As time went on, he asked her to have a meeting with him that was going to be a one-on-one meeting—which would not be unusual, you know, with the head of the public relations department—and these were scheduled in the evening, at the end of the work-day, and she was increasingly uneasy about being there. And she would say to me, "Why don't you wait for me?" Y'know, "I really don't want to be there that long or alone with him." Y'know, not inviting me to the meeting, but just asking me to remain in the building until it was time for her—until she would be able to leave.

DeOREO

Were these conversations, Ms. Jourdain, just be-tween you and Ms. Wright?

JOURDAIN

I think most of the time that she spoke to me, she spoke to me alone. My daughter was in the room once when we were discussing it.

DeOREO

Who did you talk to about Angela Wright's con-cerns about the chairman's behavior?

JOURDAIN

I don't remember speaking to anyone about it. I may have spoken—I probably did speak to my daughter.

DeOREO
It would be pretty good gossip; there would be no one else in the—

JOURDAIN
It would be gossip, but I have never been a person who was much into gossip. I was not interested in denigrating the chairman. I was not out to say, oh, he's a dog or that kind of thing.

MR. TRIS COFFIN
Hello, Rose, this is Tris Coffin from Senator Leahy's office. Can you give us a little more detail about these conversations between you and Ms. Wright, where she would tell you about the increasingly aggressive behavior.

JOURDAIN
Well, for example, I was in my office, and she would come in and she would close the door. And once she was—once she was crying—

COFFIN
Okay, slow down—

JOURDAIN
She is a very strong woman. She is not the kind of female that cries, you know what I mean?

COFFIN
Yes, I see. If you could just recall the first time—

JOURDAIN
I don't remember the first. You know, we are talking

about events that happened a long time ago. I can give you snapshot impressions, but I can't tell you which snapshot came first.

COFFIN
Okay.

JOURDAIN
I am sitting in the office, she walks in, slams the door and says, "Do you know what he said to me? Do you know what he said to me?" And I said, "No, what did he say to you?" Because it had gone on before. And I think at this point it had something to do with her legs.

COFFIN
What would he say?

JOURDAIN
I think it was like, "Oooh, you have very sexy legs," or something like, "You have hair on your legs, and it turns me on," or something like that. I thought it was nutty, you know what I mean? And it was that, but it was very unnerving to a young woman who was sitting there hearing that.

Then there was a conversation about her bra size, and there was a conversation about a dress that she wore. I don't know why that was a dress to be commented on; it wasn't a skin-tight, knit-type dress.

Sometimes she laughed about it. Sometimes it got on her last nerve. Sometimes it happened so much it was like, "You won't believe this, what he said now," y'know?

COFFIN

You mentioned earlier something about the chairman coming by Ms. Wright's house. Could you tell me about that, please?

JOURDAIN

Well, she called me up and told me that he had had the nerve to show up at her house and come in and sit down and make himself at home.

COFFIN

Can you tell me what happened step by step?

JOURDAIN

I cannot tell you step by step on anything that happened six years ago. My recollection is that it was very cold out, not the time of year when people are out for a walk and would just drop by somebody's house.

MELISSA RILEY

Ms. Jourdain, I am Melissa Riley, and I am with Senator Strom Thurmond's office. After Ms. Wright became upset about Clarence Thomas's comments, what advice did you give her?

JOURDAIN

As I remember the situation, I said to her, Why don't you sit down and just discuss it with him? I know that she had said to him, had made it clear to him that she did not welcome these advances, and I said, "Just stay firm with it, just don't let him think you are giving in to it, that there's any kind of possibility of any kind of a relationship."

RILEY

After Ms. Wright conveyed these comments to you, did you attempt to go to other women and say, "Has he made this type of comments to you?"

JOURDAIN

I did not do that. I did not feel I should discuss her business or his business with other staff members. I would never have said to anyone else on the staff that the chairman was saying these things.

RILEY

Did you consider them inappropriate?

JOURDAIN

I—yes, I did consider them inappropriate, and I did not feel it would help him at all in the delegation of his duties to have women knowing that he was saying these things.

RILEY

Okay. I guess—lastly, do you have a sense—and I hope I don't misstate this—why Ms. Wright is coming forward? Motive is the question. Do you have a sense of why she is coming forward now?

JOURDAIN

Yes. Based on what I know about her, I would tend to believe—no, I don't tend to believe, I absolutely believe—that she heard this young black woman on the television being raked over the coals, as though this experience she was having was completely impossible, that a person in Clarence Thomas's position, black or white, would not have done this, and that this woman was somehow coming from left field with some malicious agenda. And having had a similar experience, I believe that Angela would have felt it her bounden duty to go on the record saying: "This is what happened to me."

When the interview with Jourdain ended, staff members told her that she would probably have to come over to the Capitol to testify. At the same time, other aides were telling Angela Wright that she would be called to testify soon. But the evening wore on and on, and neither woman was ever called. Two days later, the nomination of Clarence Thomas to the United States Supreme Court was confirmed.

HILL *VS.* THOMAS, EPILOGUE ONE

The following exchanges took place during and after a broadcast of Nightline *just after the Thomas hearings. The guests were National Public Radio's Nina Totenberg, who had gotten a couple big scoops about Thomas, and Republican Senator Alan Simpson, who was one of Thomas's staunchest defenders and one of Hill's most strident vilifiers.*

The first volley during the program was fired by Simpson. "What politicians get tired of," the senator

said, "is bias in reporters. Let's not pretend your reporting is objective here. That would be absurd."

"I don't know who's telling the truth here," Totenberg replied, talking about Hill and Thomas. "But I do
know that I do not appreciate being blamed just because I do my job and report the news."

According to witnesses, after the program was over,
Simpson came up to Totenberg "rapidly," waving papers that he said included the Code of Ethics of the So-
ciety of Professional Journalists. "Nina," he said,
"those things I said were not said lightly. I meant
everything."

"You big asshole," Totenberg replied. "Fuck you. You
are so full of shit. You are an evil man."

"Nina, you love to dish it out, but you sure don't
like to take it."

"I don't have to listen to this shit," said Totenberg.
"You're a bitter and evil man, and all your colleagues
hate you." Later, Totenberg denied part of this comment. "I never told him his colleagues hated him—I
wouldn't know."

HILL VS. THOMAS, EPILOGUE TWO

Another of Thomas's defenders was Senator Orrin
Hatch. The Republican from Utah was the one who
suggested that Anita Hill had lifted her "pubic hair on
the Coke can" reference from an obscure passage of
The Exorcist. Soon after the hearings, Hatch was interviewed live by Bill Bonds of Detroit's WXYZ-TV.

"I have to say to you, sir," an unexpectedly feisty
Bonds began, "just as an American from the Midwest,

that frankly that was kind of an embarrassing spectacle. Do you regret that that went on?"

"It was a tense, difficult process, as it should be," the professionally unctuous Hatch replied. "And it was made worse because of one dishonest senator who leaked raw FBI data—"

"Senator," Bonds interrupted, "you guys leak all the time."

"No, that's not true."

"Who are you trying to kid? You guys leak stuff all the time."

"Let me just say something," Hatch argued. "That's not true."

"Yes it is."

"No, not FBI reports from the Judiciary Committee. I've been there fifteen years, I know what's going on there."

"There are guys who say you've been there too long," Bonds said.

"That could be," Hatch said, quickly absorbing the personal shot. "In fifteen years, I have not seen leaks of FBI reports because they contain raw data."

"Okay," Bonds said sarcastically, "your conduct was great. You guys all look terrific; 250 million Americans are really proud of Senator Orrin Hatch and all the rest of you guys."

"I'm not, I'm not—"

"You did a marvelous job," Bonds went on. "You never made the country look better. Let me ask you something: What are you going to do if you find out six months from now that Clarence Thomas, who you've just made into a saint, is a porno freak?"

"Don't worry, we won't," said Hatch. "But I'll tell

you this: If you're going to interview us in the future, you ought to be at least courteous. You're about as discourteous a person as I've ever, ever interviewed with. I don't like it, and I don't like what you're doing. I go through enough crap here in Washington, I don't have to go through it with you. Let me tell you something—"

"No," replied Bonds, "let me tell you something—"

"No, you tell yourself something. I'm tired of talking to you." Hatch then removed his microphone and walked away.

"Okay, fine," Bonds called after him. "I'm tired of talking to you. See you later."

"It Was a Strange Moment"

IN 1979, JOHN LENNON BEGAN COMPILING *his memoirs. He did that by sitting in front of a tape recorder and engaging in a mental process somewhere between ruminating and reminiscing, turning the recorder on and off, speaking about the things that interested him, stopping when he got bored. Some of those tapes have been played in public; the first of them never has.*

JOHN LENNON
The fifth of September, 1979. Tape one in the ongoing life story of John Winston Ono Lennon. I'll talk about 9 Newcastle Road, because that's the first place I remember. . . . Red brick, front room, never used, curtains always drawn, picture of a horse and carriage on the wall. . . . This is boring. . . .

Just, I was just remembering the time when I had my hand on my mother's tit. . . . It was when I was about fourteen, took the day off from school. . . . We were lying on her bed, and I was wondering if I should do anything else, you know? It was a strange moment, because I actually had the hots, as they say, for some rather low-class female who lived on the opposite side of the road. But I always think I should have done it. Hmm. Presuming she would have allowed. . . .

By the way, Mother was wearing a black angora, short-sleeved, round-necked sweater. Not too fluffy, maybe it was that other stuff, cashmere, that's it, right, cashmere. Soft wool, anyway. And I believe that tight dark-green yellow-mottled skirt. Hey, ho. [*Sighs.*]

"I Took These Photos,
I Put Them on My Mantel,
and I Went On with My Day"

A COUPLE OF YEARS AGO, PEOPLE WERE astonished to hear that Woody Allen and Mia Farrow were splitting up. The cause of the separation was Woody's affair with Soon-Yi Previn, who was Farrow's eldest daughter and, by extension, Woody's quasi-step-daughter. That would have been complicated enough for most households, but the Allen-Farrows did not inhabit most households. (Name another family that has therapists for everybody, including, as testimony revealed, the dog.) And so things turned nasty. Farrow accused Allen of being a child molester and sued him for custody of their three children. The hearing took place in Manhattan in 1993. Allen spent two days on the stand, but the most remarkable testimony came at the close. His lawyer asked him a final question, one that seems simple and rather obvious. But Allen's answer was not.

ATTORNEY
Last question. Can you tell the court why you are seeking custody of your children?

WOODY ALLEN
Why I'm seeking custody? I'm seeking custody of the

children for—because I believe firmly and with all my heart that their best chance in life—their best chance in life is if I am the custodial parent of the children. I do not want to take the children away from Mia, that's not my intention at all. I have said to her many times, I want us both to fully participate in the bringing up of the children, that's all I want. I don't want to make her unhappy.

I—look, let me go back for a second, if I can. After five years—when Satchel was born, after five years of, of a kind of joyless, sexless relationship in which Mia and I parented the children together, she was the, the dominant one, because she—they lived at her house and I—as you've heard. I felt, after that period of time—I'm not saying this, and I won't give you all the details of it, but rightly or wrongly, I started to have a relationship with Soon-Yi. She was a grown person. My perception—and I say this—rightly or wrongly—I can't, I wouldn't put my life on this, but I—my perception of Mia's household—as I perceive it, was—over the years—five—there were a number of kids from—some biological, some from different parts of the world. I felt that Soon-Yi was fifteen years older than Dylan, seventeen years older than Satchel. I—and again I say this, I'm not, I'm not saying that I'm right about this, I'm just saying my perception of this was, this was not a traditional household at all, as I went through it. A household with many children, with an adoption that could come and go, with kids from different parts of the world, with kids sleeping in bunk beds!

I did not—my reading of the—my own personal reading, from going through it for years, was that—because you asked me this question earlier—did I not conceive of this as a sister relationship between the kids? My perception of this was this was not a traditional thing. This was—I'm not saying this correctly, I don't mean it exactly like this—it was more like a foster home feeling. There were a lot of kids there that had been adopted, and I—and Soon-Yi was, you know, an older person, and I did not perceive it—and again, I could be wrong about this, I'm not saying that I'm right—I did not perceive this as, as traditionally, a traditional family, in a—you know.

At any rate, I began a relationship with Soon-Yi. I fell, I fell in love with her. Perhaps this was wrong, not wise, whatever, you know? I don't know what to say about it. I did love her—I do love her, you know? And I did not conceive of this at that time the way one would conceive of it in a more traditional family. I didn't see it that way. I was a man who lived out of the house and never lived there. She was an older person, much, much older than the kids.

And, you know, I was in an, in an unfruitful relationship, in which the only thing that Mia and I had in common is that we worked and we parented the kids.

And so, this relationship began. I began it—I mean, it's my responsibility, I began it—and in a very, very brutal and unpleasant way, it was discovered. I did not, by any stretch of the imagination, want that to happen. By any stretch of the imagination. I lived alone, I took these photographs of Soon-Yi, this was an adult transaction with two consenting adults. We had started a relationship. This was something that we wanted to do. I did this, I placed these photographs on my mantel, and went out. And as I say, I lived by myself. But in a very painful way they were discovered by Miss Farrow the next day.

I had just started the relationship with Soon-Yi. I had just started it, and if, if it had turned out that she and I—she was home on her Christmas vacation, and if it had turned out, then she and I were going to sit down and say, "Look, we're serious about this with one another." At some point, I would have sat down, or Soon-Yi would have sat down, or we all would have sat down, both of us with Mia, and discussed this, and said, "What shall we do about this? Nothing at all? Shall we do something? Can something be done?" But what happened was suddenly and completely surprising to me. It was discovered. And in a way that I, I appreciate was extremely painful to Mia, I understand that. I did not want that to happen.

My behavior over the last thirteen years has not been to make Mia miserable. I have been, I think, very nice with her, and very giving with her. I'm not a cruel person, I don't want to make her unhappy. This was an accident. You know, I took these photos, they came out of the silly Polaroid, I put them on my mantel, and I went on with my day. This was not a big deal in my life. Coincidentally, the next day Mia came. I was shooting a film, so when that happened—and as I say, I appreciate her hurt under those circumstances, her shock and all that.

The thing was, I had just started a relationship with Soon-Yi, just really not even two weeks prior to that, and I only had a couple of times with her, I was with her only a couple of times. If—what happened was

Mia just went so explosive at that time that there wasn't any—there was no way of containing this. I mean, when it happened, what, what would be my, my fondest wish—I realize it's idealized—would be for Mia to say, "My God, this is horrible, you hurt me so badly, this is awful," and that it would be something that the three of us—Soon-Yi, Mia, and myself—would resolve in some way.

And it could be resolved any number of ways. I mean, I, I'm not suggesting how to resolve it. It could have been, you know, get our lawyers together instantly, get me away, I never want to speak to you again, I never want to see my daughter again, whatever. You know, I understand, I allow for any of the spectrum of things. But there was a sudden cosmic explosion, and there was nothing that could be done after that. . . .

And I was there at the time! I was there that day—I was there any number of days—I was on the telephone. Now, I'm not trying to abdicate any kind of responsibility for this. I'm not saying my selection of Soon-Yi was a brilliant selection or a wise selection. And I don't offer up the prior five years as any kind of an excuse or anything. I can only say that I felt genuine feelings for Mia, still do, and I have been willing—all along, I said to Mia, "Please, whatever we do, let's—" It's possible that if Mia and Soon-Yi and I had sat down together and somewhat at least kept it secret—maybe sit down together is too rational to think about—but if the three of us had come together privately, privately, without any therapists involved, with just us, it's possible we could have resolved this.

But the children were used by Mia in the most shameless, degrading way, right from the start. . . . I kept saying, Let's try and do this civilized, let's not involve the little children in this, or minimize it. I screwed up, I caused this thing to happen, okay. But don't seek vengeance on me through the kids. Seek it through the courts, seek it—hit me continually if you want to. I don't know what to say, let's just leave them out of it. But that didn't happen. There was constant, constant utilization of the children all the time. Culminating in the August fourth allegations, where poor Dylan has been put through this horrible thing. . . .

Now I've given you a long-winded answer here. I think that, that I did make a mistake, an error in judgment here. I have my own feelings about it, but I do think, I do think that. But I think the response to it has been absolutely degrading and criminal. And right up until two days ago, I suggested the notion of let's shake hands, let's stop hostilities instantly. I'll tell the kids that, you know, you're a good mother, and we argued with each other, we had problems. You tell them that, that, y'know, I love them and I'm a good father, and they should love me. . . .

I don't know what else I could have done in this situation, given the fact that I did fall in love with Soon-Yi. There were many ways that it could have been handled other than this. I just want to take full responsibility for my participation in it and to say that I think given what has occurred—I don't know. I honestly don't know if Mia could ever—because it's now been fourteen months since this happened and the rage has not abated one iota, there is not an inch of flexibility or concern with the children. And so I'm saying, I feel that if the children lived with me, that—and that if the children lived with me, my posture would be that fifty percent of the time, they would see their mother, that I have no problem with that.

I would tell them to love their mother. I would give them, you know, the most generous life, education, responsible therapy that's necessary. Soon-Yi and I have spoken about this many times, and both of us have agreed any number of times that our situation is definitely secondary to the best interests of the children. Whatever responsible doctors—the kids' doctors—told us to do, we would do, in relation to the best interests of the children.

If you ask me—personally—I would say the children, the children adore Soon-Yi, they adore me, they would be delighted—if you asked me this personally—I would say they would be delighted and have fun with us, being taken places with us. But I don't want to give you my amateur opinion on that. That's how I feel, and I know it counts for very little.

I feel if the children are with me, they will be responsibly educated. They will be—they will be—their day-to-day behavior will be done in consultation with their therapist. Their therapist can be chosen responsibly by the court, can be chosen in collaboration with Mia and myself, but I would be very good. I would not have them evaluated for an indiscriminate amount of time, I would get them into treatment, and, as I said, I would encourage their love for Mia. I would encourage their time spent with Mia. I would not say she's going to hell, or you can't love your mommy, or anything like that. I would be generous about it. . . . If it were possible—and helpful for the kids, beneficial for the kids—for Soon-Yi to be included in that in any way whatsoever, that's fine. You know, I, I want only what's correct for them. Soon-Yi wants only what's correct for them.

So all I can say is, my—from where I sit—you'll think it's self-serving, but from where I sit, my, my prognostication for them with me would be more generous and loving, in relation to Mia. I would welcome a two-parent, coparenting thing. . . .

I've said before that every single financial aspect of this, I agree. I have always agreed, and agree again, to undertake in every way. I will pay for every single thing in relation to the children, for their entire—until they're grown up! Until they're out of graduate school! I mean, anything. Their doctors, their college, their lessons, anything. You know, I just want a good life for them, and I feel that I can better provide that.

Now, if you—if it was demonstrated to me that it would be provided just as well from Mia, or better from Mia, then fine, I'll go with that. I want what's right for the children. That's all I can say.

ATTORNEY
No further questions.

"I Use It for a Special Dance"

FROM THE DAY OF THEIR WEDDING WE'VE *heard that the marriage of Michael Jackson and Lisa Marie Presley was in trouble. That's too bad. It had been reassuring to know that all that weirdness had consigned itself to a single gene pool. But even if the marriage isn't long, it's been useful, if only as a distraction. You'll recall that just before his wedding, Michael was in the news because certain accusations had been made against him. Authorities have since decided not to press any criminal charges, but the investigation was by no means fruitless. Consider, for example, this Q and A. Asking the questions is Larry Feldman, the attorney for the boy suing Jackson. Responding is Blanca Francia, Michael's former maid. Also present, and from time to time speaking, are Jackson's attorneys, Howard Weitzman and Johnnie "O.J. Did What?" Cochran.*

LARRY FELDMAN
  Did Mr. Jackson ever call himself "doo doo head"?

BLANCA FRANCIA
  Yeah. And he will tell me sometimes "doo doo head" too.

FELDMAN
  He'd call you "doo doo head"?

FRANCIA
   Yeah.

FELDMAN
   How about "apple head"?

FRANCIA
   No, I never hear that.

FELDMAN
   Was it a term—do you know what, like, a term of
endearment is? Would he affectionately use that term
"doo doo head," or would he use it to criticize somebody? I'm trying to get a sense of how he would use
the word "doo doo head."

FRANCIA
   Yeah. Like—like, he will say, "Oh, I'm hungry and I
don't know what to eat. Maybe some doo doo." He
will say that and—or he will say to me, "This is doo
doo."

FELDMAN
   Now, the children that you saw in bed with Michael
Jackson, were they always boys?

FRANCIA
   Yes.

FELDMAN
   Did you ever see any little girls in bed with Michael
Jackson?

FRANCIA
No.

FELDMAN
Did you ever see any adult women in bed with Michael Jackson?

FRANCIA
No.

FELDMAN
Did Michael Jackson have a monkey?

FRANCIA
Yes, he had a monkey.

FELDMAN
And was the monkey at Jackson's house in Encino?

FRANCIA
Yes. Bubbles.

FELDMAN
Bubbles? And where did Bubbles sleep in Encino?

FRANCIA
In his bedroom in a cage.

FELDMAN
And did Bubbles wear any kind of diaper or anything?

FRANCIA
Yes.

FELDMAN
Was he bare-chested too?

HOWARD WEITZMAN
I'm sorry, that's naked. Bare-chested is [the word we'll use] for the monkey.

JOHNNIE COCHRAN
That's naked [for him], bare-chested for the monkey.

WEITZMAN
That's what they *wear*. The *fur* is their clothes.

COCHRAN
I see.

FRANCIA
Diaper.

FELDMAN
Now, Miss Francia, you told us before that you would buy Mr. Jackson's underwear for him, right?

FRANCIA
Yes.

FELDMAN
Did there ever come a point when you started realizing that Mr. Jackson was missing underwear? Would he be losing it someplace?

FRANCIA
Yes. I keep buying and buying a lot of underwears,

and sometimes he will have so many. Sometimes he will have like sixty.

FELDMAN
   Sixty? Six zero?

FRANCIA
   Yeah. Sixty. Fifty or sixty underwear.

FELDMAN
   In his drawer.

FRANCIA
   In his drawer. And it was, like, *a lot*. And then I say, "You have a lot of underwears." And he say, "Well, because sometimes they get too tight."

FELDMAN
   Happens to us all.

FRANCIA
   Uh-huh.

FELDMAN
   Did there ever come a time when Michael Jackson was missing underwear?

FRANCIA
   Yes.

FELDMAN
   Where the supply would go down.

FRANCIA
  Go down.

FELDMAN
  And you'd have to go buy more.

FRANCIA
  Yeah. There were times when I notice that he only wear—like, only five he will use, and the other ones were put aside. And he would look for the special ones he wanted to wear. And I remember—well, I don't know if I'm supposed to say it.

FELDMAN
  What? Go ahead.

FRANCIA
  That he had one with a little pocket in the front, and he asked me what did I think about that.

FELDMAN
  And what did you say?

FRANCIA
  I say, "Well, I don't know." And he say, "Well, it's just that I use it for a special dance."

FELDMAN
  The underwear with the pocket?

FRANCIA
  With the little pocket.

COCHRAN
  This is a pocket? Or a puppet?

FRANCIA
  Pocket.

COCHRAN
  Pocket?

FRANCIA
  Uh-huh.

FELDMAN
  Did he tell you what special dance he was doing?

FRANCIA
  No, no. He say—he say sometimes he will throw
them away.

FELDMAN
  So sometimes literally the underwear will disap-
pear.

FRANCIA
  Yes.

FELDMAN
  And he would tell you he threw them away.

FRANCIA
  Yes.

FELDMAN
  And then you'd go out and get new ones?

FRANCIA
Uh-huh, yes. And he says—one time he says, "Don't get surprised if you see any dirty underwears, because sometimes I can't go to the bathroom, and I will just go in my underwear."

FELDMAN
So you'd see his underwear stained sometimes?

FRANCIA
Yes.

FELDMAN
From urinating?

FRANCIA
From urinating, yeah.

FELDMAN
Or from, maybe, semen?

FRANCIA
I wouldn't—

FELDMAN
Would you know the difference? Could you tell?

FRANCIA
I can't tell the difference, because I just picked them up and put them with my dirty laundry, and that's it. I just don't want to find out.

FELDMAN
You don't want to find out?

FRANCIA
   Yes.

FELDMAN
   You would know the difference, but you never tried
to find out.

FRANCIA
   Yes.

"Bitch Set Me Up"

IN JANUARY 1990, VIEWERS OF THE NETWORK news programs were treated to an unusual sight: one of the best-known American mayors smoking crack and then being arrested by agents of the FBI. The mayor, of course, was Marion Barry of Washington, D.C. He had been lured up to a room on the seventh floor of the Vista Hotel by his ex-girlfriend, Rasheeda Moore, a former model. Unbeknownst to him, however, she had run afoul of the law. In order to escape punishment, she decided to cooperate with the FBI in its longtime pursuit of Barry. The several-second video of the mayor sucking on the crack pipe is well known, as are the scenes of the agents charging in to bust him. But the camera kept running after that, and that portion of the tape is less well known.

MARION BARRY
Goddamn, I shouldn't have come up here!

FBI AGENT
You have the right to remain silent. Anything you say can be used against you in court.

BARRY
I'll be goddamned.

AGENT
  You have the right to—

BARRY
  Yeah, I know all that.

AGENT
  —talk with a lawyer for advice—

BARRY
  Piss me off.

AGENT
  —before we ask you any questions. You may have a
lawyer with you—

BARRY
  Got a setup—

AGENT
  —during questioning.

BARRY
  Goddamn, got a setup.

AGENT
  If you cannot afford a lawyer, one will be appointed
for you before any questioning, if you wish. If you decide to answer questions now without a lawyer present—

BARRY
  Shit!

AGENT
   —you will still have the right to stop answering—

BARRY
   Bitch set me up.

AGENT
   —at any time, until you talk to a lawyer.

BARRY
   She set me up. I'll be goddamned.

AGENT
   Do you understand your rights?

BARRY
   Yeah. She set me up like that, I'll be—

AGENT
   Okay.

BARRY
   Got me set up. Ain't that a bitch! Motherfucker! I shouldn't have come up here.

AGENT
   Mr. Mayor, I'm going to ask you if you want to waive your rights, and sign the form that you understood your rights—

BARRY
   I want to call my lawyer right now. I'll be goddamned. I got fucked up here with this goddamn bitch,

setting me up like this. Set me up. Ain't that a bitch!

AGENT

We know about your past cardiac history with narcotics, so we're just—

BARRY

Naw, naw, she, she, that bitch, that bitch did that to me.

AGENT

—we're just going to make sure that you're physically sound and not suffering any kind of health problems, that's all.

BARRY

Son of a bitch. She kept, kept pushing me—

AGENT

Just stand calm—

BARRY

I'm all right. That goddamn bitch!

AGENT

—and we'll have them take a quick look at you, take your blood pressure, your vital signs—

BARRY

That goddamn bitch!

AGENT

—make sure you're okay. All right?

BARRY
That, that goddamn bitch. That goddamn bitch. Tricked me to get me up here, son of a bitch. And you know, tricked me like a motherfucker. Can I call my wife?

The emergency medical technicians arrive to check on Barry.

TECHNICIAN
How do you feel?

BARRY
I feel fine, except I'm pissed off.

TECHNICIAN
Are you on any medications at this time?

BARRY
Naw, man. Shit. Goddamn bitch. Ain't that a bitch?

TECHNICIAN
Okay, just, just relax, just a minute, please, we, we've got to—

BARRY
Goddamn bitch. I should have stayed downstairs. Goddamn . . .

TECHNICIAN
It'll be just a second. Deep breath.

BARRY
Elaborate goddamn trap, I tell you.

TECHNICIAN
Just let me take it one more time, okay?

BARRY
That goddamn—that goddamn bitch tricked me into this shit. I should have—I should have stayed down in the motherfucking lobby like I decided to.

TECHNICIAN
Sir, I understand that possibly you've been exposed to something that could be adverse to your health.

BARRY
Well, I don't know what the hell it was. I know I was tricked. Goddamn bitch.

The mayor now has to wait for a squad car to take him to central booking at a police precinct in his own city. A District of Columbia police officer tries to comfort him.

COP
We didn't really want this to happen. Really.

BARRY
I didn't want it to happen, either. I should have—if I had followed my fucking instincts tonight, I'd have been all right. I should have stayed downstairs. Bitch kept insisting I come up here. Goddammit.

AGENT
It's been a traumatic experience. But this, too, shall come to pass.

TECHNICIAN

Sometimes it's better. Sometimes it's for the better. Really, healthwise, you know—

BARRY

Oh, you're assuming I got—you're assuming I got a problem.

Even with the videotape as evidence, the jury seemed to feel that the issue of entrapment—If you're going to use sex as bait, couldn't you get lots of men to do nearly anything?—was a real one, and they convicted Barry of only cocaine possession. He was sentenced to six months in prison, from which he emerged, he said, with a new sobriety and a new outlook on life. Four years later, he ran for mayor, asking the voters to forgive and forget. Remarkably enough, they did.

"Hello?"

BEFORE MCI AND SPRINT, BEFORE CELLULAR *phones, before all the present-day wonders of telecommunications, diplomacy was more difficult. It is 1976. The president of the United States, Gerald Ford, is speaking on the phone to the president of Egypt, Anwar Sadat.*

GERALD FORD
President Sadat?

ANWAR SADAT
Hello, this is President Sadat.

FORD
How are you this morning? [*Small pause*] President Sadat, I wanted to call you and congratulate you on the great role you played in the negotiations that have culminated in this agreement.

SADAT
Hello?

FORD
Unfortunately, I don't hear you too well, Mr. President. I hope my conversation is coming through more

clearly. [*Pause*] Let me express most emphatically on behalf of my government the appreciation for your statesmanship, despite adversity and criticism, the spirit with which you have approached the need for an agreement. I look forward to continuing to work with you.

SADAT
Hello?

FORD
Hello. Can you hear me, Mr. President?

SADAT
No, I can't hear you very well.

FORD
I know that you and I recognize that stagnation and stalemate in the Middle East would have been potentially disastrous, and your leadership in working with Secretary Kissinger and with the Israelis, all of us are most grateful for.

SADAT
Hello?

FORD
Yes, I can hear you, President Sadat. I hope you can hear me, Mr. President.

SADAT
Ah, President Ford, hello.

FORD
 I don't hear too well, Mr. President.

SADAT
 President Ford speaking?

FORD
 Yes, this is President Ford.

SADAT
 Go ahead, please.

FORD
 The connection, unfortunately, is not too good for me
to hear your comments. Let me say, if I might, despite
the difficulties, that Mrs. Ford and I hope that Mrs. Sadat and you and your children will visit the United
States sometime this fall. I regret that I can't hear. The
connection is very bad. I hope you can hear me and
my comments from the United States.

SADAT
 Hello?

FORD
 Hello, Mr. President.

SADAT
 Hello, Mr. President.

FORD
 I can hear you better now, sir.

SADAT

Mr. President, I hope you and your family are well.

FORD

I am feeling very well, Mr. President. I hope you are, too.

SADAT

I want to thank you for your personal message.

FORD

Mr. President, I couldn't hear every word distinctly, but I got the thrust of your kind comments and your encouraging words, and I can assure you that we will work with Egypt, not only in seeing that the agreement is implemented with the spirit, as well as the letter.

SADAT

Mr. Ford, I am looking forward to this visit with you and Mrs. Ford and your family. I also assure you that we will accept this agreement as a further step towards a successful and peaceful conclusion. I consider it a turning point in the history of the country.

FORD

I, unfortunately, could not hear as well as I would like the last comments you made. The connection here, apparently, is not as good as I hope you have there.

SADAT

I hear you quite well.

FORD
Have a good day. Henry will be there shortly, I understand.

SADAT
I am waiting for him.

"It's Very Simple. The Media Feeds on Itself"

OKAY, WHAT PERSON DO YOU THINK OF *when we say, "a thousand points of light"? How about "the vision thing"? How about "throwing up on the Japanese prime minister"? While George Bush will be known for all these things, he's going to be best remembered for the splendid little war he conducted in 1991 against Iraq and its dictator, Saddam Hussein.*

But Bush wasn't always interested in going to war against Saddam. In fact, until Saddam invaded Kuwait, Bush wanted Saddam to be our friend. Those were the days, you may recall, when Saddam was stockpiling chemical weapons, and had bought a huge gun barrel that could fire a shell a thousand miles, and was saying things like, "I swear by God we will let our fire eat half of Israel." Bush was apparently willing to indulge a little hotheadedness—if it didn't go too far. To try to fend that off, in the spring of 1990, mere months before we were at war, Bush asked some of his friends in the Senate to visit Saddam, to try to calm him down. Among the delegation were Senators Alan Simpson and Bob Dole. Their conversation was transcribed by Radio Baghdad.

ALAN SIMPSON

I'm glad to have the opportunity to speak with you, Mr. President. I enjoy meeting with frank and direct people. I'm from Wyoming, and it's difficult for us in the Wild West—the cowboys—to understand that when we lose a case sometimes, we do not lose our life. That's why we called President Bush yesterday. We told him that our visit to Iraq will cost us dearly, as it will make us lose popularity, and so many people will attack us for visiting Iraq. But President Bush told us, "Go. I want you to go. Tell him we have perspective." The things you said about Israel are the same things we in the United States have said about the Soviet Union. Who will strike first? Who will press the button first? Who will turn half the United States into a fireball? Now we have perspective. Now we are going to reduce our military budget, and Secretary of State Baker and Foreign Minister Shevardnadze go fishing together.

You talk about democracy. Democracy is a very irksome and confusing thing. I believe your problem is with the Western media, not with the U.S. government. It's because you're isolated from the press and the media. The press is spoiled and conceited. All the journalists consider themselves brilliant political scientists. They do not want to see anything succeeding or achieving its objectives. My advice is that you allow those bastards to come here and see things for themselves.

SADDAM HUSSEIN

But if the U.S. government is not responsible for propagating the bad stories about me, how then was such a huge amount generated in such a short time?

SIMPSON

It's very simple. The media feeds on itself. One of them eats part of the other. A front-page story in *Newsweek* is taken by another reporter and published by him, and so on.

BOB DOLE

There is something I would like to say. Since you invited reporters to come here, why don't you ask them to go to the place where they say biological weapons are produced? Challenge them to prove that you speak nothing but the truth.

SADDAM

I assure you, we will lose nothing if we ask them where the biological weapons are, and also ask them to lead us to them. But we know these media organs—as you do. They are like a spoiled child. If a child is given a sweet in response to his desires and cries, he will continue to cry all the time.

DOLE

The media have a role to play, and I do not think the media are wrong all the time.

SADDAM

Neither are they always right.

DOLE

In fact, I always say they are wrong all the time, especially when they attack me. But I'm not talking about myself.

SIMPSON

You know, Mr. President, I practiced law in a small town for eighteen years, during which fifteen hundred divorce cases came my way. Every one of those cases was brought on by the coldness of the partners. There was a breakdown of communication. Self-righteousness, pride, and opinionatedness led to separation. It is highly important, Mr. President, that even while we argue and yell at each other, we must keep up the dialogue. Otherwise, the world will be shaken by an enormous divorce.

I am not a peaceful person; I like argument and struggle. A while back, President Bush said he hated broccoli, since his mother used to force it on him. The American media has written extensively on this anecdote. Some newspaper articles argued that President Bush, after all, is not the wimp he was made out to be.

That's where the transcript ends. Four months later, Bush was comparing Saddam to Hitler. Bush, of course, is no longer president. Saddam, of course, still is.

"This Stuff Is Just Floating Around"

SPIES BY DEFINITION ARE A CLOSEMOUTHED group, and traitors are even quieter. Thus it was something of a bonanza in 1994 when Aldrich Ames, the high-ranking CIA official who'd sold out to the Soviets, decided to open up a little. But why not? He'd already been captured. He knew he was going to spend the rest of his life behind bars. He knew his wife, who'd also been implicated in his scheme, would be sent upriver for a long time unless he cooperated. His new best friends at the KGB had gone out of business. Talk? We're lucky he hasn't gotten his own show on CNBC. Instead, he went one-on-one with Senator Dennis DeConcini, who was then the chairman of the Senate Select Committee on Intelligence.

DENNIS DeCONCINI
Let me ask you some questions, Mr. Ames, as to motivation. When did you decide that you wanted to share information with the KGB?

ALDRICH AMES
It was in the period of February and March of 1985.

DeCONCINI
How did that come about?

AMES
I felt, I felt a great deal of financial pressure. Which I, in retrospect, I was clearly overreacting to. The previous two years that I had spent in Washington, I had incurred a certain amount of personal debt in terms of buying furniture, inexpensive furniture, furniture for an apartment. And my divorce settlement had left me with no property, essentially. I think I may have had ten thousand or thirteen thousand dollars in debt. It was not a truly desperate situation, but it was one that somehow really placed a great deal of pressure on me.

DeCONCINI
And you had remarried.

AMES
And I was planning to remarry, and I was contemplating the future. I had no house, and we had strong plans to have a family, and so with those pressures— perceived pressures—I conceived of this plan, this con game or scam, to get money from the KGB.

DeCONCINI
When you say con game or scam, did you at that time think you were not going to give them anything they could really use?

AMES
That was the plan that I carried out in April.

DeCONCINI

They were going to give you money, and you were going to give them useless information.

AMES

That's exactly right. And I saw it as a onetime thing. To get fifty thousand dollars, which, it seemed to me, would get me out of the hole, provide a kind of nest egg for the future.

DeCONCINI

Did you know who to contact?

AMES

Yes, I did. Yes, I did. I knew who the KGB resident was.

DeCONCINI

How did you make the contact?

AMES

There was a Soviet embassy officer I had been lunching with who told me to talk to another officer at the embassy, an officer concerned with arms control issues, who would perhaps be more appropriate, since I was representing myself as associated with the Intelligence Community Staff. I was using an alias. And my plan was, at our first meeting, to give him a letter to take back to his ambassador. Inside the envelope would be the name of the KGB resident.

DeCONCINI

That would give you credibility.

AMES

Yes. And in that letter, I gave them information—essentially valueless information—which I knew in their eyes would appear genuine.

DeCONCINI

What was it?

AMES

We had a report in 1984 that the KGB was going to dispatch us two false volunteers who would act as double agents. And two volunteers did appear. So I told them that.

DeCONCINI

What was their response?

AMES

Their response was very positive. They came back in May and gave me fifty thousand dollars.

DeCONCINI

Is that right? When you made the offer, you said, "This is a onetime thing," and you said, "I want fifty thousand dollars."

AMES

That's right. "I am selling you this for fifty thousand dollars. Here it is."

DeCONCINI

And they came back with fifty thousand dollars.

AMES
Fifty thousand dollars.

DeCONCINI
And at that time, you figured you were finished.

AMES
When I had got the money, I figured I was finished. And I'm still puzzled as to what took me to the
next steps. The main factor was a realization, was a
sense of the enormity of what I had done. I think I
saw the plan I carried out in April as a clever,
clever—not a *game*, but a very clever plan to do one
thing. But somehow without reckoning what it was I
was really doing. And it came home to me, after the
middle of May, the enormity of what I had done. That
I had crossed a line which I had not clearly considered before. That I had crossed a line and could
never step back. And it's very difficult for me to re-
construct my thoughts from that time. It was as if I
were in almost a state of shock. The realization of
what I had done.

But certainly underlying it was the conviction that
they'd give me as much money as I could ever use, if I
chose to do that.

DeCONCINI
You mean, continue?

AMES
That's right. So in June I gathered up from my desk
documents, cables, traffic—

DeCONCINI
Just general—

AMES
General, but reflecting virtually all of the most important cases we had. And I gave it to them.

DeCONCINI
Gave it to them.

AMES
Gave it to them. With no preconditions.

DeCONCINI
No preconditions.

AMES
I said nothing about money. I just said, "Here." In a
sense, I was delivering myself to them.

DeCONCINI
You just gave it to them.

AMES
Just gave it to them. And then throughout the summer
I continued to give them things.

DeCONCINI
And when did you get paid again?

AMES
In the early summer.

DeCONCINI
Did you have to ask for payments?

AMES
No. They just gave them to me.

DeCONCINI
They'd just call you up and say, "Here's a payment."

AMES
That's right.

DeCONCINI
And you gave them names.

AMES
New, additional names.

DeCONCINI
When you gave these names, did you realize the danger that these people would be in?

AMES
Yes, I did.

DeCONCINI
Did you rationalize, that this was not—

AMES
I didn't agonize over it.

DeCONCINI
Did it occur to you that they might be killed?

AMES
  Yes, it did.

DeCONCINI
  So after you did this, when did you go to Rome?

AMES
  In July of '86.

DeCONCINI
  And you had access to everything that came into the Rome station. Which I understand is a pretty heavy-hitting station.

AMES
  Well, I wouldn't characterize Rome station as being the center of a lot of sensitive operational activity, but the nature of the organization and the paper flow meant that a tremendous amount of material about policies and plans and resources went there.

DeCONCINI
  So you had all that.

AMES
  Yes, and I passed it along.

DeCONCINI
  And they liked having that.

AMES
  Yes, they certainly did.

DeCONCINI
How did you take the material out?

AMES
Put it in envelopes in a shopping bag and left the embassy.

DeCONCINI
You made Xerox copies. Is that what you did?

AMES
No, I very seldom Xeroxed copies.

DeCONCINI
What did you do? Did you take the originals?

AMES
I just took the originals.

DeCONCINI
I see.

AMES
I was supposed to destroy it or my secretary was supposed to destroy it. But it wound up with me. So I had this paper at my disposal.

DeCONCINI
And the information you had access to, how did you get it? Was it in a controlled security place?

AMES
It came into my in box.

DeCONCINI
Just came to your in box.

AMES
And I would just scoop it out.

DeCONCINI
And the stuff that came into your in box—if you decided, gee, there may be something else I want to know about this operation report, you could get it?

AMES
Generally. My branch basically advised other branches.

DeCONCINI
So you really had access to everything.

AMES
Yes, I did.

DeCONCINI
It came right across your desk.

AMES
Exactly right.

DeCONCINI
If there was a document that hadn't come in to you, but was referred to in the report that came into your in basket, could you go to the appropriate office and go, "I want to see it"?

AMES

I could go to that office and say, "You know, I am looking at such and such a case, and apparently there was a report, can I take a look at it?" And the person in the other office, the responsible officer, would either make a decision or consult with his boss.

DeCONCINI
Yes.

AMES

And you might get the answer "No, you've got to talk to my boss." Or they might say, "Oh, sure."

DeCONCINI

Was there ever any rumors—or reality—of lost documents within the agency?

AMES

Oh, yeah. Every time they would inventory top secret documents, you know, hundreds and thousands would turn up missing.

DeCONCINI
Would be gone.

AMES

Bureaucratic inertia and friction.

DeCONCINI
That's what it was attributed to?

AMES
Yes.

DeCONCINI
   Did anybody follow up?

AMES
   I don't know.

DeCONCINI
   You don't recall anything?

AMES
   No, uh-uh. Files would always get lost. You would go and look up a file on a Soviet official or a project—

DeCONCINI
   And couldn't find it.

AMES
   It would have disappeared from the face of the earth.

DeCONCINI
   And nobody—

AMES
   And everybody would religiously search, and look, and it might turn up years later. Or it might not.

DeCONCINI
   Does this impress you as being an awfully sloppy operation?

AMES
   Of course. Of course. The KGB had tremendous difficulty understanding it. They were worried to death about my security.

DeCONCINI
Yeah, how you could get—

AMES
They'd say, "How can you get this stuff—"

DeCONCINI
And not be detected.

AMES
Yeah! They couldn't understand how I could do this without damaging my security.

DeCONCINI
Yeah.

AMES
But eventually, they came to believe me when I said, "Well, this stuff is just floating around."

DeCONCINI
You were surprised when they arrested you.

AMES
I was completely shocked and surprised.

"Of Course We Want to Have Fun!"

AMONG THE MORE THRILLINGLY INCONSE-
quential stories of the last few years was the saga of
Heidi Fleiss, the pediatrician's daughter who became
the so-called Hollywood Madam. Fleiss was the
woman, allegedly, whom actors and studio executives
would call upon for female companionship, in much
the same way as they would call upon, say, Wolfgang
Puck for goat cheese pizza (except Puck, of course, has
never been accused of felony pandering for feeding
people). A key player in the tale was Heidi's ex-
boyfriend Ivan Nagy (pronounced EE-vahn NAHJ), a
former TV-movie director. He allegedly got her into
the business and was allegedly her partner. Once they
separated, he became Heidi's nemesis. The next conversation is between Nagy and a young woman named
Julie, who had worked for Heidi. They are apparently
talking about going into business together.

JULIE
Well, let me ask you this. How is Heidi going to feel
about all this? I mean, how would she feel? I don't
know—I guess that's none of my business—

IVAN NAGY
No, it's your business. Because if we do anything together, anything that affects me affects you. And you
are more than correct in asking the question. Basically,
I am not concerned with how she feels about it. Okay,

that's number one. Number two, as we start doing this I will do everything within my know-how to get her operation to come to a standstill. So between you and me, she will be out of business. Or she will be in business at an extremely reduced stature, with only a few girls. I can effect all this.

JULIE
You can effect all this?

NAGY
Yes. I can actually tell you that if what I have in my mind goes into operation, Heidi Fleiss will be arrested—there is no question about it. You understand that?

JULIE
Yeah.

NAGY
The only question is—is it going to happen on the seventh of February or the ninth of March?

JULIE
I see, yeah.

NAGY
Or the fifteenth of April. That I don't know. That I really don't know.

JULIE
But you know for sure that's going to happen?

NAGY
It's going to happen. For sure. She will be arrested.

JULIE
That's too bad. It's really too bad.

NAGY
It's sad. It's very, very sad.

JULIE
So you think you're going to call my friend Cookie and talk to him? Just, you know, approach it like—

NAGY
I will approach it my way.

JULIE
Approach it your way, yeah.

NAGY
I'm going to say to him, "Look, the time has come, let's talk. Here are my problems, Cookie. My problem is that I only understand the high end of the business."

JULIE
You?

NAGY
Me, Ivan. I only understand how to run a shop on Rodeo Drive. There's nothing wrong with having a shop on Main Street. Nothing wrong with it. A big dis-

count store. As a matter of fact, some of those people may make more money than the ones on Rodeo Drive. I don't want to go to Main Street. I don't know how that functions. I want to operate on Rodeo Drive. You follow me?

JULIE
Right. No, I totally follow you.

NAGY
And I think he's a very bright guy. His—his assets are terrific.

JULIE
He has what?

NAGY
You have assets. Personal assets.

JULIE
I do?

NAGY
No, Cookie.

JULIE
Cookie?

NAGY
I am now referring to Cookie. I'm paraphrasing my speech to Cookie. Okay?

JULIE
Ooooh, okay.

NAGY

You have terrific assets and I'd like us to do this together and I think we can do it very well. You need to
make a decision whether you want to continue on
Main Street or would you like to move to Rodeo Drive.

JULIE

Right, yeah. He'd understand that. I think.

NAGY

If you want to move to Rodeo Drive, let's give it a shot.
But I'll expect you to listen to me. Not only listen, but
when we come to an agreement, we will all act on that
agreement. And an agreement doesn't just mean that at
the end of a coffee session that everybody goes back out
and does whatever the fuck they want to do. 'Cause if
that's how you want to be, I can't. I don't want to do it.

JULIE

Right, okay. I agree.

NAGY

Correct. And look, I also want to have fun. I mean,
obviously I'm not doing it—

JULIE

Of course we want to have fun. That's the whole
point.

NAGY

That's the whole point of it, isn't it?

JULIE

Yeah. But there is a business part of it that has to be
fixed and ironed out and everything else.

NAGY
And can I tell you something? The better the business, the more fun you have.

JULIE
Exactly.

NAGY
Because let me tell you something. There's nothing more fun than to have a girl crawl all over you after she's just finished turning three fifteen-hundred-dollar tricks.

JULIE
Yeah.

NAGY
See what I'm saying to you?

JULIE
They make you feel good, too.

NAGY
It's so much easier. You need so much less chatter. The girl's on autopilot.

JULIE
No, no, I totally understand what you're saying. It's just that, you know, to me, I would think the difficulty in getting all these clients is having the kind of girls that they want.

NAGY
Heidi's got them.

JULIE

Heidi's—yeah, yeah, but—Heidi's got them, yeah, she's got them.

NAGY

So what's the big deal?

JULIE

Well, I mean—those are hers, you know?

NAGY

Who would be hers? They're not labeled hers. John has hired girls from Heidi, and he's hired girls from Alberto. Okay?

JULIE

Oh, so it's not like they belong to somebody.

NAGY

No, and the clients don't belong to anybody. What you gotta understand about a trick, he's the same as a drug addict, okay? Every so often, they need drugs, and they will buy the drug from whoever's got it.

JULIE

Right.

NAGY

Okay, they may be used to calling one guy, but if that one guy's not around, or he doesn't have drugs on him—

JULIE

—or the kind of drugs that he wants—

NAGY
You got it. They're not gonna quit doing drugs, they're gonna call the next guy.

JULIE
Right.

NAGY
Okay. Same thing. These guys are hooked on pussy.

JULIE
Hooked on pussy.

NAGY
They're not interested in Heidi. They're only interested in Heidi because right now—

JULIE
She's supplying them with pussy.

NAGY
She's supplying them the pussy.

JULIE
Right.

NAGY
When she stops supplying them, or—

JULIE
—someone else supplies them better pussy—

NAGY
  Then they switch.

JULIE
  They switch.

NAGY
  You got it. And that's where I can help. Take John
the driver. I give you John the driver, he drives a limo
for every big shot who comes into town. And the first
thing they say to John is "John, how do we get laid?"

JULIE
  Right.

NAGY
  And he says, "Hah! I got it—Julie!"

JULIE
  Oh, Julie.

NAGY
  The best, the newest, the best.

JULIE
  The newest and the best.

NAGY
  You got it.

JULIE
  Sounds good to me.

NAGY
So then you pay off John. Every time he recommends somebody, give John a hundred bucks.

JULIE
Give him a hundred bucks every time I send a girl with him?

NAGY
Sure, why not?

JULIE
And then the next time they come to town, they don't have to ask John, they already know to call me.

NAGY
And, one better—

JULIE
They tell their friends.

NAGY
They go home, they say to their friends, "By the way, you go to L.A., you say hello to Heidi. That's passé, passé. Now it's Julie." And in a year, your phone is not gonna stop ringing.

JULIE
Sounds good to me.

NAGY
That's how it works. I know John the driver longer than Heidi has a cunt on her. You understand?

JULIE
Yeah, I see. Ivan, like I say, it sounds great. I just think you need to talk to Cookie.

NAGY
And if I can't work anything out, you know, what can I tell you?

JULIE
Well, we'll talk. We'll see. Let's just see what happens. Anyway, call him. And then you can call me. You know?

NAGY
All right. After I finish talking with him—

JULIE
Call me.

NAGY
I will.

After Heidi's arrest in 1993, both Nagy and Julie were arrested on pandering charges as well. Nagy maintained his innocence, and the charges were dropped. Nagy, however, is not above making money off Fleiss and sex; he now sells a pornographic CD-ROM, entitled Heidi's Girls.

"All You Need to Do Is Let Me Know"

THERE ARE PEOPLE ONE WOULDN'T MIND having as an ex. "Really?" you wouldn't mind people asking you. "You dated Audrey Hepburn?" At best, your former boyfriends or girlfriends make you seem formerly attractive, or interesting. (Look how much mileage the conservative moralist William Bennett gets from having once dated Janis Joplin; would that she were alive to tell her side of the story.) At worst, they make you seem human.

Then there are the people—for instance, people familiar with the RECORD CONVERSATION *function on their phone answering machines—whom you really don't want to break up with.*

In September 1991, the governor of Arkansas, Bill Clinton, a man preparing a run for the presidency, gets a call from his old friend, Gennifer Flowers, an Arkansas state employee who is trying to get a career going as a nightclub singer.

GENNIFER FLOWERS
The reason I went to my mother's is that my mother gets a phone call. This has all happened to me last week. I'm going to tell you, I am a nervous wreck.

BILL CLINTON
Your mother got a call?

FLOWERS
My mother gets a call from a man who won't iden-
tify himself, and tells her, "Boy, you ought to be really
proud of your daughter." And goes on and on, and of
course my mother now, you know, is not one—she's
not gonna take this from this guy, and she says, "Now,
look." You know, she's tellin' him, "Don't call." And he
says, he says to her, "Well, I think she'd be better off
dead." And hangs up the phone. Are you there?

CLINTON
A long-distance call, do you think?

FLOWERS
My mother said it sounded like— Now here's the
thing, Bill. My mother's name—it's not Flowers.

CLINTON
So somebody had to go—

FLOWERS
Somebody—yeah, somebody had to know to ask for
that name.

CLINTON
Republican harassment trying to break you and me.

FLOWERS
And I just—I don't know. I'm, of course, I, I'll have to
tell you, I'm about to cry, because my nerves at this

point, after this week. And I'm a pretty strong little lady, but I have been through a lot.

CLINTON
But the people at the club were from *A Current Affair?*

FLOWERS
That's what John said. I just headed for the door. I said, "Leave me alone, this is absurd." He started sticking that thing and I knew—I mean, that's a private club. I didn't think they would follow me. But here's the thing: I have to have these singing jobs to survive. I'm only making seventeen-five on this job, Bill.

CLINTON
How can I help?

FLOWERS
I don't know anybody anywhere, to speak of. I have mixed emotions about this, because I consider this my home—

CLINTON
I mean, this is just crazy. There's not going to be any stories. No one has said anything.

FLOWERS
The only thing that concerns me at this point is the state job.

CLINTON
Yeah, I've never thought about that. But as long as

you say you've just been looking for one— If they ever
ask if you've talked to me about it, you can just say no.

*They talk again a few weeks later. By this time, Clinton
has announced that he's a candidate for president. He's
in Washington, and, as busy as a candidate can be, he
nevertheless finds time to call his old chum the nightclub singer in Little Rock.*

FLOWERS
   Hello?

CLINTON
   Gennifer?

FLOWERS
   Yes.

CLINTON
   It's Bill Clinton.

FLOWERS
   Hi, Bill.

CLINTON
   Hey, I tried to call ya. I can't believe I got ya.

FLOWERS
   Well, when did you try to call me?

CLINTON
   Last night. Late.

FLOWERS
Well, I was here.

CLINTON
Did you take your phone off the hook?

FLOWERS
Well, I did. I—well, I've been getting these hang-up calls, and at one point, I took my phone—I, well, I didn't take it off the hook, I just, uh—

CLINTON
Turned it off?

FLOWERS
Yeah.

CLINTON
Oh, that's what it was. I called. I started calling as soon as I got home last night, and I called for a couple of hours.

FLOWERS
Well, sorry I missed you.

CLINTON
I was afraid I screwed up the number or something, and I kept calling.

FLOWERS
Well, good. Good. The reason I was calling was to tell you that, uh, well, a couple of things. Uh, this last Wednesday, someone got into my apartment.

CLINTON
Hold on a minute.

FLOWERS
Okay.

CLINTON
Okay, I got it.

FLOWERS
Are you in Little Rock?

CLINTON
No.

FLOWERS
No.

CLINTON
I'm going to be there. I'm in Washington now, and I'm going to Dallas, but then I'm coming to Little Rock. So—somebody broke into your apartment.

FLOWERS
Well, yeah. Well, there wasn't any sign of a break-in, but the drawers and things— There wasn't anything missing that I can tell, but somebody had—

CLINTON
Somebody had gone through all your stuff.

FLOWERS
  Had gone through my stuff.

CLINTON
  But they didn't steal anything?

FLOWERS
  No. No, I had jewelry in here and everything. It
was still here.

CLINTON
  You think they were trying to look for something
on us?

FLOWERS
  I think so. Well, I mean, why, why else?

CLINTON
  You weren't missing any kind of papers or anything?

FLOWERS
  Well—like what kind of papers?

CLINTON
  Well, I mean, any kind of personal records, or
checkbooks, or anything like that? Phone records?

FLOWERS
  Do I have any?

CLINTON
  Yeah!

FLOWERS
Unh-unh. I mean, why would I? You—you usually call me. And besides—who would know?

CLINTON
Isn't that amazing?

FLOWERS
Even if I had it on my phone records—oh, well, I guess they might be able to say, "Oh, well, you were in Washington on this date, and maybe at that number," and connect that, but—

CLINTON
Well—

FLOWERS
See, you've always called me. So that's not—

CLINTON
I wouldn't care if they—you know, I— They may have my phone records on this computer here, but I don't think it—that doesn't prove *anything*.

FLOWERS
All right, darling. Well, you hang in there. I don't mean to worry you. I just—

CLINTON
I just want to know these things, and if I can help you.

FLOWERS
Well, when you can help me is if I decide I want to get the heck out of here.

CLINTON
All you need to do is let me know.

FLOWERS
Because I don't know—I don't know where to turn. I really don't. I mean, my contacts have just sort of fizzled in Nashville. It's been a long time, and I don't know anybody.

CLINTON
I'll help you.

FLOWERS
Well, I'll be back in touch. And, oh—will you let me know if you know anything I need to know about?

CLINTON
I will.

FLOWERS
Okay?

CLINTON
Good-bye, baby.

A few weeks after this, just before the New Hampshire primary, Gennifer Flowers, having been paid by the tabloid newspaper the Star, *went public with the claim that she and Clinton had had an affair, using this highly suggestive but hardly conclusive tape as proof. But Clinton went on 60 Minutes, won the nomination, and won the election. Still, the stories wouldn't go away, and just before Christmas 1993, some Arkansas state troopers alleged that they helped him pursue and* cover up extramarital liaisons. Naturally, reporters wanted to know more. "So," one pressed him, "none of this ever happened?"

"I have nothing else to say," the president replied. "We—we did—if—the—I—I—the stories are just as they have been said. They're outrageous, and they're not so."

"I've Never Said
It Was Good for Someone"

FINISH THIS SENTENCE: "WARNING: THE SUR-geon General has determined that cigarette smoking is . . ." If you said, "dangerous to your health," you're like most people. On the other hand, if you said, "re-ally, really profitable," then you're one of the few peo-ple who have what it takes to be a tobacco company executive. In 1993, a group of flight attendants, as well as the survivors of some who are dead, sued the coun-try's cigarette manufacturers, contending that exposure to smoke in flight caused their illnesses and deaths. As part of the case, the plaintiffs' attorney, Stanley Rosen-blatt, deposed several tobacco industry executives. Here is their sworn testimony.

First is Rosenblatt questioning William I. Campbell, the president and chief executive of Philip Morris USA.

STANLEY ROSENBLATT
Does cigarette smoking cause cancer?

WILLIAM I. CAMPBELL
To my knowledge, it's not been proven that cigarette smoking causes cancer.

ROSENBLATT
What do you base that on?

CAMPBELL

I base that on the fact that, traditionally, there is, you know, in scientific terms, there are hurdles related to causation, and at this time, there is no evidence that— they have not been able to reproduce cancer in animals from cigarette smoking.

ROSENBLATT

Have Surgeon Generals of the United States concluded that cigarette smoking causes cancer?

CAMPBELL

Yes.

ROSENBLATT

Why don't you accept their conclusions? I mean, you don't have a scientific background. What information do you have, or what literature or in-house memos have you received, that cause you to conclude they are wrong?

CAMPBELL

I have not concluded they are wrong. I said that it has not been proven. . . . The argument is that, you know, the causal relationship in animals has not been proven.

ROSENBLATT

Well, I'm not talking about animals. I'm talking about human beings. If somebody is a two-pack-a-day smoker for twenty years, and he gets lung cancer, and every medical person is satisfied that he got lung cancer because he smoked, you still say it is not proven.

CAMPBELL
  That is correct. That is what I'm saying.

ROSENBLATT
  Can you name a single scientist or medical doctor
who will publicly say that he or she doesn't believe it's
been proven that cigarette smoking causes cancer?
Somebody not employed by the tobacco industry, or
who never got money from the tobacco industry?

CAMPBELL
  I can't answer that.

ROSENBLATT
  Dr. Antonia Novello, the former Surgeon General,
recently wrote in the *Journal of the American Medical
Association,* "Tobacco is the only product that, when
used as directed, results in death and disability." What
is your answer to that?

CAMPBELL
  I don't know.

ROSENBLATT
  You don't know.

CAMPBELL
  It has not been proven.

ROSENBLATT
  She says, "We must expose the seduction of our children by the tobacco industry, and work pro-actively to
counter its messages and techniques. More than a mil-

lion children start to smoke in the U.S. every year. That is three thousand per day. Ten percent start smoking by the fourth grade." Do you have any information to counter those figures?

CAMPBELL
No, we don't.

ROSENBLATT
[*Reading from a warning that is printed on all packs of cigarettes and that appears in cigarette advertising*] "Smoking by pregnant women can result in fetal injury, premature birth, and low birth rate." Do you agree with that?

CAMPBELL
"May result." That's a statement by the Surgeon General, not our statement.

ROSENBLATT
But it's on your product.

CAMPBELL
Yes. We accepted the language.

ROSENBLATT
Is it accurate? As far as you're concerned, as president of Philip Morris, is it accurate?

CAMPBELL
I don't know.

ROSENBLATT
Do you agree with the findings of the Environmental Protection Agency, which say that secondhand smoke causes about three thousand lung cancer deaths a year among nonsmokers?

CAMPBELL
I do not believe statistics support that statement.

ROSENBLATT
They concluded that environmental tobacco smoke presents a serious and substantial public health problem.

CAMPBELL
I have not seen evidence to support that.

ROSENBLATT
So you don't agree that environmental tobacco smoke causes cancer in healthy nonsmokers?

CAMPBELL
I do not agree with that.

ROSENBLATT
And you don't agree with the conclusion that passive smoke increases the risk of pneumonia and bronchitis in children.

CAMPBELL
I don't have the knowledge to support that.

Later, Rosenblatt deposed Andrew H. Tisch, the chairman and chief executive of the Lorillard Tobacco Company.

ROSENBLATT
Does cigarette smoking cause cancer?

ANDREW H. TISCH
I don't believe so.

ROSENBLATT
Based on what?

TISCH
Based on my understanding of the scientific and statistical evidence that's been published.

ROSENBLATT
What is your understanding of that evidence?

TISCH
That there's been no conclusive evidence that's been presented that convinces me that cigarette smoking causes cancer.

ROSENBLATT
Since you, as chairman and chief executive of Lorillard, believe that it hasn't been proven that smoking causes lung cancer, heart disease, and emphysema, why do have that on your packages?

TISCH
Because this is what is required of us as a matter of law.

ROSENBLATT
  You have to do it.

TISCH
  That is correct.

ROSENBLATT
  If you didn't have to do it, you wouldn't do it.

TISCH
  Not necessarily.

ROSENBLATT
  As far as you're concerned, Mr. Tisch, as chairman and chief executive of Lorillard, this warning on the package that says smoking causes lung cancer, heart disease, and emphysema is inaccurate. You don't believe it's true.

TISCH
  That's correct.

ROSENBLATT
  Because if you did believe it was true, in good conscience, you wouldn't sell this to Americans, or for that matter foreigners, would you?

TISCH
  That's correct.

ROSENBLATT
  Mr. Tisch, you're a father, right?

TISCH
  Yes.

ROSENBLATT
How old's your oldest?

TISCH
He's fifteen.

ROSENBLATT
Does he smoke?

TISCH
Not to my knowledge.

ROSENBLATT
If he did, to your knowledge, what would you do
about it?

TISCH
Seeing as he's fifteen years old, I would probably
not be very happy. He's not old enough to make that
decision.

ROSENBLATT
Would you prohibit him from smoking?

TISCH
Yes.

ROSENBLATT
Why?

TISCH
Because smoking is an adult choice.

ROSENBLATT
What's wrong with a fifteen-year-old smoking if smoking doesn't have any adverse health consequences?

TISCH
I'm not saying that it doesn't. I said I'm not convinced of it.

ROSENBLATT
So your position is that smoking may very well cause lung cancer, heart disease, and emphysema, but you're not convinced that it does.

TISCH
That's correct.

ROSENBLATT
When will you consider your kids adult enough to make the decision?

TISCH
At eighteen.

ROSENBLATT
So when your kids turn eighteen and it becomes their practice to smoke a pack and a half a day and you were aware of it, what, if anything, would you say to them?

TISCH
That's a hypothetical question. I'm not sure what I would say to them at that point.

ROSENBLATT
You certainly don't contend that smoking is good for anybody, do you?

TISCH
I've never said it was good for someone.

ROSENBLATT
When your children are old enough, would you prefer that they smoke or not smoke? Or are you entirely neutral?

TISCH
I would prefer that they not smoke.

Finally, Rosenblatt deposed Bennett S. Le Bow, the chairman of the Brooke Group, which owns the Liggett Group.

ROSENBLATT
Does your wife smoke, Mr. Le Bow?

BENNETT S. LE BOW
Yes.

ROSENBLATT
What is her brand over the years?

LE BOW
Marlboro.

ROSENBLATT
Strictly?

LE BOW
As far as I can recall.

ROSENBLATT
  Yes?

LE BOW
  Yes.

ROSENBLATT
  Doesn't even smoke your brand.

LE BOW
  Please—that hurts.

ROSENBLATT
  Does your daughter smoke?

LE BOW
  Yes.

ROSENBLATT
  Did you ever try to say to your wife or daughter, "It's
really not a good idea to smoke"?

LE BOW
  No, not at all.

ROSENBLATT
  Why not?

LE BOW
  Because I never felt a need. They're adults. They
make their own decisions. . . .

ROSENBLATT
  Is it fair to say that since you're satisfied you have a

legal right to sell cigarettes, you have never really explored or studied the issue of whether or not cigarettes cause disease.

LE BOW
That is absolutely correct.

ROSENBLATT
So if I asked you, does smoking cause lung cancer—

LE BOW
I'd say I don't know.

ROSENBLATT
And you really don't care, because you're selling a legal product.

LE BOW
Correct.

ROSENBLATT
Okay; are you familiar with the warnings that appear on your products?

LE BOW
Not in detail. I have read them on occasion, obviously.

ROSENBLATT
Okay; does any warning on the package of one of your products mention lung cancer?

LE BOW
I don't know for sure.

ROSENBLATT
So there's no point in my questioning you as to what it says about lung cancer.

LE BOW
I don't know them in detail. I have seen the warnings. I don't recall the exact words of the warnings.

ROSENBLATT
The warning that mentions lung cancer is one sentence.

LE BOW
Okay, if you say so.

ROSENBLATT
And if you don't remember the exact wording, fine, but can you tell me what it says?

LE BOW
No, I can't. I don't remember.

ROSENBLATT
Does it say smoking may cause lung cancer, or does it say smoking causes cancer?

LE BOW
I have no idea.

ROSENBLATT
Now, if there wasn't this lawsuit, and if, you know,

you and I were friends, and we were just talking, and I said, y'know, "You're in this business, and I'm very antismoking. I would really like you to be convinced that cigarettes are dangerous. I can get together for you, anytime you ask, twenty leading authorities in the world on the issue of whether cigarette smoking causes lung cancer and other diseases, and you can have as long as you want to question them, because I would really like you to be convinced." Would you avail yourself of that opportunity?

LE BOW
   No.

ROSENBLATT
   Why not?

LE BOW
   I have no interest.

ROSENBLATT
   You've never read a Surgeon General's report dealing with the issue of smoking and health, correct?

LE BOW
   Correct.

ROSENBLATT
   If I mention a report that got a lot of attention, the Environmental Protection Agency's report on smoking and health, would that ring a bell with you?

LE BOW
   I read something about it in the newspapers, yes.

ROSENBLATT
Do you remember even generally what you read?

LE BOW
There was some claim about secondhand smoke, you
know, causing various diseases. That was the claim.

ROSENBLATT
You never read it?

LE BOW
Never read it.

ROSENBLATT
And I assume you don't have any knowledge on the
subject?

LE BOW
I have no knowledge.

ROSENBLATT
No knowledge?

LE BOW
No.

ROSENBLATT
And no interest in acquiring any knowledge.

LE BOW
That is correct.

ROSENBLATT
As I understand your position, generally, that kind of

issue is someone else's battle, and you're going to do your thing, as long as it's legal to do it.

LE BOW
   That is correct.

ROSENBLATT
   And make as much money as you can while you're doing it.

LE BOW
   I'm a businessman.

Not the Norton Anthology

POETRY, SOME SAY, IS AN ESOTERIC CRAFT, A
dead art. But they are wrong. Poetry survives. The
muse lives.

In fact, as it turns out, the muse lives part of the year
in the District of Columbia. Presenting the seven-term
congressman from Brooklyn, Mr. Major Owens, who
delivered the following odes in no less a place than the
floor of the House of Representatives. From the Congressional Record:

HOORAY FOR THE WHIPS

Are we PAC asses for the classes
Or strong mules for the masses?
I got a whip
You got a whip
All of God's children got a whip
Whip for who
Whip for what
Do your duty
Please beat my butt
Whip hard
And make it pay
We need education oats
We need health care hay.

INCEST CITY

The public has a right to know
Full meaning of charges
Made by mad Ross Perot
Cocktail power's finest hour
Is after session.
Never mind financial disclosures;
Confess your intimate connections.
Who's whose mama,
And what's your sister's married name?
Insider trading of political information
Is still a legal game.

MILK THE SACRED COWS

No pain, no gain
The CIA budget is still insane
Seawolves are obsolete
An extinct species
Not worth their weight
In biodegradable feces.
Seawolves devour reason
Advocate intellectual treason.

WIMPS WITHOUT VISION

Budget Committee wimps
Bowing to burned-out military pimps
Smiling at scientific whores
From NASA space station doors

Of course, the poetry revival is not just a Washington thing. On the opposite coast, passionate young men have also taken to expressing themselves in verse. The following poem is by one of America's most prominent young writers. His name is Mickey Rourke.

DRAMA

Like An Actor With Amnesia
Or A Director Without A Penis
You Made Me Cry
Like An Orphaned Baboon
Chained to the Dyke Saleslady
At Bloomingdale's
In N.Y.C. at Xmas Time.

Eliot. Lowell. Rourke. And Sheen—Charlie Sheen is another very masculine young actor who's turned to verse. His works, too, project the special angst that derives from living life as a young, handsome, celebrated, modestly talented multimillionaire.

AFTER A FULL-BODY MASSAGE
FROM GINGER IN L.A.

There's a goat in my ass
Living mainly on grass.
They say the creature was stolen
Yet he feeds on my colon.

Now a sampling from the oeuvre of another young ac-

tor-poet, Robert Downey, Jr. The directness and fertile imagery of this work strikingly parallels that of the Sheen work.

GORILLAS ON MY DICK

Gorillas on my dick
Gorillas on my dick
Sigourney's beaver's an underachiever
Gorillas on my dick.

E.T., the extra-testicle
E.T., the extra-testicle
E.T., the extra-testicle
Gorillas on my dick.

I'm gettin' my act together
And takin' it up the ass
I'm gettin' my act together
And takin' it up the ass
I'm playin' a ball called tether
And spackling up my gash
With gorillas on my dick.

The marvelous thing about poetry, of course, is that one doesn't have to be a politician or an actor to write it. This next selection is by Andrew Wylie, a certified member of the American literary establishment. He is not, however, a writer but a literary agent, the representative of such authors as Norman Mailer, William Burroughs, Salman Rushdie, and Martin Amis. In

1972, *however, Wylie published a collection of his own poetry. Here is a selection.*

THIGHS

thighs
on my neck
I suck
the clit

When this collection was published, one critic, Richard Williams, wrote, "Poetry died so that people like Wylie can flourish—and that's great!"

"This Is Not the Funny Part Yet"

THE COURSE OF TRUE LOVE IS NEVER AN easy one. After all, how in this day and age do you prove how much you really love someone? Perhaps, if you're like Marla Maples, you sign a self-abnegating prenuptial agreement with the highly leveraged casino operator who fathered your newborn child. Or if you're like Ted Danson, you dress up in blackface in order to roast your lover, Whoopi Goldberg, at a Friars Club lunch, which is what Danson did one day in 1993, causing a tremendous uproar. Here is just the start of his actual remarks. See if you think they were worth it.

TED DANSON

I'm here today, my darling, because you're one of the most elegant women I know. When we're walking around on the streets, people come up to us and say, "Thank you, Whoopi, thank you, oh God, thank you!" This is not the funny part yet!

You are royalty. You really are. I'm honored to walk at your side in life. I hope that we can all salute you, since there is nothing I enjoy in life more than making you laugh. So—go, Whoop!

Before I get into my thing, I wanted to say that this morning, as I was shaving and wondering what I was going to say this afternoon, Whoopi was giving me a blow job. And all of a sudden, I looked down, and I said "Aw, c'mon, Whoop! Don't nigger-lip it!" I came to discuss a problem here, ladies and gentlemen! Please now! And we laughed and we laughed and we laughed. I know, I'm prepared for arguments, but I got to tell you, black chicks sure do know their way around a dick. But in fairness, white girls get toys for Christmas. . . .

But we get a lot of press. A lot of press. I love being in the tabloids. In fact, we had our first fight, with all our "problems," we had our first fight this morning. There's this new picture we're going to be doing for Disney called *The Nigger Lovers*. And Miss Diva here insists on playing the nigger! I said, "C'mon, Whoop! You always play the nigger. Just because you did the nigger nun doesn't mean you get to play the nigger all the time. Let someone else play the nigger. How hard can it be?" . . .

Moments later, Danson turned to face the honoree and said, "I do believe I remember you saying, 'I dare you.'" Then, a few days later, Ted and Whoopi went on a radio show to attempt a little spin control, saying how proud they were of what happened, inasmuch as it had inspired a national debate on the subject of interracial relationships. And a few weeks after that, Ted and Whoopi had split up.

"That's *Riotous*, You Greaseball"

SOME OF YOU MAY BE THINKING THAT loose lips are a recent phenomenon, that not long ago people knew how to keep quiet. Not true. Lips have been loose at least as long ago as . . . well, as long ago as 1953. That was the year that Jerry Lewis and Dean Martin got together to record some radio commercials for their eminently forgettable hit The Caddy *(or, if you happen to be from France,* Le Caddy*).*

DEAN MARTIN
  Hi, everybody, this is Dean Martin—

JERRY LEWIS
  And Jerry Lewis—

MARTIN
  And we'd like to tell you all about our latest and funniest picture for Paramount.

LEWIS
  Of course you mean *The Caddy.*

MARTIN
  You'll love Jerry and me in *The Caddy.*

LEWIS
  Take my word for it: *The Caddy* is the most hilarious

picture we've ever made. Come and join the fun! See Paramount's *The Caddy.*

MARTIN
Yeah, *The Caddy!* [*Long pause; then, to the control room*] Is that all right, you cocksuckers?

LEWIS
How was that, you shitheel?

MARTIN
Was that readin' it?

ENGINEER
I'm with ya.

LEWIS
Next. You still rolling?

MARTIN
You still rollin'?

ENGINEER
All right, start.

MARTIN
You can cut that bit out.

ENGINEER
I will.

LEWIS
Okay.

MARTIN
Now, this is Dean Martin—

LEWIS
—and Jerry Lewis, asking you to see our newest and
funniest picture to date.

MARTIN
Of course, you mean *The Caddy.*

LEWIS
You bet I do.

MARTIN
Crazy, man, crazy.

LEWIS
No doubt about it, Dean, this is the funniest picture
we've ever made. No kidding, folks, we're sensa-
tional! Take my word for it! Come on and join the fun!
See Paramount's *The Caddy.* It'll make you shit.

MARTIN
Cut out "make." Hi, this is Dean Martin—

LEWIS
—and Jerry Lewis, with a reminder to see our
newest and funniest motion picture ever: *The Caddy.*

MARTIN
Oh, he's right, folks. Come on and join the fun, and
the most right-u-ous ninety minutes of howls—

LEWIS
   Rightuous? Where the fuck do you see *rightuous?*
That's *riotous,* you greaseball!

MARTIN
   This is a religious Martin and Jerry Lewis. Five fuck-
ing lines, and we can't get through it. Come on. This is
Dean Martin—

LEWIS
   —and Jerry Lewis, with a reminder to see our
newest and funniest motion picture ever: *The Caddy.*

MARTIN
   Oh, he's right, folks. Come on and join the fun, and
the most wonderful ninety minutes of howls and gags
you ever saw.

LEWIS
   We'll be seeing you in Paramount's *The Caddy.*

MARTIN
   Yep, *The Caddy.*

LEWIS
   With a big cock on it.

"We Have No Usable Calls"

CAN ONE EVER GET ENOUGH OF TOM SNY-
der? *The NBC show from the '70s and early '80s, the*
local TV news anchor stints on the way up and on the
way down, the radio shows of the early '90s—if we
could, we would possess a vast collection of Snyderi-
ana. Back before his current, Letterman-ordered come-
back as a talk show host on CBS, Snyder hosted a live
show on CNBC. The first guest on his first show in
1993 was the circa-1960 satirist Mort Sahl. The cam-
eras, of course, rolled during the commercials, and
here's what the postmenopausal entertainers talked
about when they weren't *on the air.*

First break:

TOM SNYDER
Do you go out?

MORT SAHL
Yeah, but with less and less frequency. It's really
tough.

SNYDER
Isn't it awful?

SAHL
There aren't any women!

SNYDER
I had a note in my mailbox today: "Dear Mr. Snyder, I'm a neighbor of yours who would very much like to meet you. My name is et cetera et cetera. If you're interested, my number is such and such. Hint: slim blonde." [*Pause*]

SAHL
You gonna call?

SNYDER
No.

SAHL
No.

SNYDER
No!

SAHL
You've been there.

SNYDER
I've been there.

Pause. Sahl is playing with a credit-card-size calculator-like object.

SAHL
I'm doing your biorhythms.

SNYDER
Oh, right, I used to have one of them.

SAHL

You're emotionally critical today. [*Pause*] No, I tell ya, women—the values of women. Last night I was at a screening of *Chaplin* at Jimmy Komack's house. [Komack was the creator and executive producer of *Chico and the Man*. Ed.] The picture ends, and there's an epilogue that says "The FBI kept a 1,900-page file of Charlie Chaplin's surveillance." And this dame says to me—

SNYDER

What?

SAHL

"Do you know what that costs?"

BOTH

Ha ha ha ha ha ha ha ha ha ha ha ha!

Second break:

SAHL

You know, you were very sporting about all your successors and everything. But aside from that, they don't talk!

SNYDER

Who?

SAHL

The guys who succeeded you! I mean, they don't talk! None of them talk!

SNYDER

[*Agreeing*] They don't talk.

SAHL
I mean, weren't you more combustible at forty-four
than Jay Leno is?

SNYDER
Yeah. Yeah!

SAHL
I mean, come *on*, fellas! [*Pause*] You know, I would
never say this on the air, but heterosexuality is dying. If
you listen to ABC radio, Peter Tilden is always talking
about his hair. His hair! And if he breaks an appointment at the salon, it bugs him. A guy!

SNYDER
Yeah. Yeah!

SAHL
You don't want to sit and drink beer with him!

SNYDER
[Radio talk show host Michael] Jackson, too! Unctuous!

SAHL
Aw, he's awful!

*Third break. An attractive woman comes onto the
set to apply makeup to Snyder.*

SAHL
Bush went to his office today.

SNYDER
[*To the woman*] You know, Kelly, they're probably at

home saying, "Gee, Snyder's makeup is getting a little thin on his forehead, they better get some more on." They're out there, they're stoned, they're zonked. [*She finishes and quickly moves away. Without missing a beat, he picks up the conversation with Sahl.*] Where? In Houston?

SAHL
Yeah, he went to his office in Houston.

SNYDER
What is the matter with him?

SAHL
With his dog.

SNYDER
He's got this beautiful house in Kennebunkport by the sea, and he goes down there to some putz rented house in Houston to live. What a schmuck!

SAHL
Next door to Jerry Weintraub.

Fourth break:

SAHL
What are you driving, Tom?

SNYDER
I drive an STS.

SAHL
They're great, aren't they?

SNYDER
  They're wonderful.

SAHL
  They really did it.

SNYDER
  They really did it.

Before long, the show went to a call-in format. Our tape shows Snyder during yet another commercial break, sitting on a stool, wiggling around, preparing to talk to some viewers.

SNYDER
  This phone book is very uncomfortable.
  [*Pause*]

TECHNICIAN
  [*Offstage*] We have no usable calls.

SNYDER
  We what?

TECHNICIAN
  At the moment, we have no usable calls.

SNYDER
  [*Cranky*] What does that mean, "no usable calls"?

There's no answer, just a long pause.

Ah, the dreaded words "no usable calls."

Kelly the makeup woman reappears and applies some powder.

Are you going to start using rubber gloves on me?

She does not answer. She finishes.

Thanks, Kel.

She walks away, departing through an exit behind him. As she walks away, he swivels around completely to watch her go. He then turns back around and, staring into the middle distance, begins singing to himself.

Unforgettable,
That's what you are.
Darling, it's just incredible
That you find
My cock so edible—

He stops and stares into space.

"I'm No Longer on Prozac, Bitch"

EVEN WHEN ROCK AND ROLL IS BEING ITS most corporate, a little bit of bona fide rebelliousness can't help but sneak in. Or perhaps we mean that even when Roseanne (i.e., the artist formerly known as Roseanne Arnold and previous to that known as Roseanne Barr) is dressed up, a little tastelessness can't help but sneak in. Either way, these exchanges between Roseanne and the famously right-wing veejay Kennedy were edited out of the official broadcast of the 1994 MTV Music Video Awards. The first is an excision from Roseanne's opening monologue.

ROSEANNE
I saw Kennedy backstage, and I told her, "I know Martha Quinn, and you are no Martha Quinn." Then she asked me to leave, because she was blowing Rush Limbaugh.

Before long, Kennedy joined New York City Mayor Rudy Giuliani in presenting the MTV Viewers' Choice Award. Unbeknownst to the mayor, Kennedy pantomimed fellatio on camera as he was speaking. Later on, another veejay, Bill Bellamy, asked Kennedy if she wanted to respond to Roseanne's remarks.

KENNEDY
Yes, I was backstage before the show, giving Rush

Limbaugh a hummer. That's [*Again she simulates fella-tio*], in case you guys didn't know. I have to concede to Roseanne. He said she gives a much better blow job. So: the Prozac's working.

Roseanne, of course, got the last word.

ROSEANNE
I would like to respond to Kennedy. I'm no longer on Prozac, bitch. Rush Limbaugh told me you swallow.

"I Was Elected in 1989"

LONG BEFORE RONALD REAGAN DISCLOSED *that he was suffering from Alzheimer's disease—long, long before—our greatest modern president was famous for his casual attitude toward facts. There was, for example, the big White House meeting on urban issues, when Reagan greeted one of his own cabinet officers, Secretary of Housing and Urban Development Samuel Pierce, by saying, "Hello, Mr. Mayor, nice to see you again." Then there was the occasion when he addressed Liberian President Samuel Doe as "Chairman Moe." But perhaps his most interesting excursion into forgetfulness was his performance during the 1990 perjury trial of Admiral John Poindexter, Reagan's former national security adviser. Poindexter had been indicted for lying to congressional committees investigating the Iran-contra affair, and he called Reagan as a witness.*

ATTORNEY
   Good morning, Mr. President.

RONALD REAGAN
   Good morning.

ATTORNEY
   A little background. When were you elected president?

REAGAN
I was elected in 1989. In November 1980. Took office on January 20, 19—or January 21, 1981.

ATTORNEY
Prior to that, you were governor of California?

REAGAN
Yes. I was elected in 1966 and served eight years.

ATTORNEY
And before that, you were in the movie business.

REAGAN
Yes, although there—well, no. I was going to reverse things. Prior to working in the movie business, I was a sports announcer in radio.

ATTORNEY
When did you meet Admiral Poindexter?

REAGAN
The only recollection I have is when he was deputy to the national security adviser, and I was already in office. Now, if there was some prior time or meeting or gathering where we met, I don't recall.

ATTORNEY
Do you have some general recollection of the Iran-contra event?

REAGAN
Yes. It was a covert action taken at my behest.

ATTORNEY
Have you familiarized yourself with the charges against Admiral Poindexter?

REAGAN
No, I haven't, I must confess.

ATTORNEY
They are based on two events: one, letters he sent to a congressional committee; and two, testimony he gave about a shipment of Hawk missiles. Do you recall anything about either of these events?

REAGAN
I only recall learning at some point that there had been a shipment of Hawk missiles by Israel to Iran. But that's about the extent of my recollection.

ATTORNEY
How often did you meet with Admiral Poindexter?

REAGAN
Usually every working day.

ATTORNEY
What portion of your schedule is devoted to national security affairs?

REAGAN
I couldn't recall definitely. Obviously, a major part.

ATTORNEY
Can you describe what you understood the Iran initiative to be?

REAGAN
A group of individuals, citizens of Iran, journeyed to a third country. Contact was made with us that they wanted to discuss with is how better relations between Iran and the United States could be secured. And so a delegation of ours—I believe it was all from the National Security Council—journeyed to meet with these people.

ATTORNEY
Was this journey made by Robert McFarlane and others in approximately April or May 1986?

REAGAN
I can't recall, and I can't set down the dates.

ATTORNEY
But you are referring to McFarlane's trip?

REAGAN
No.

ATTORNEY
Do you recall being first briefed on this situation at Bethesda Naval Hospital with McFarlane and Don Regan?

REAGAN
I recall that I had visits every once in a while there at the hospital. I have to tell you, I really can't recall what those visits were about. Nothing tremendously earth-shattering, according to my memory, but I'm afraid I wasn't maybe quite up to pinning things down.

ATTORNEY
What about a later meeting at the White House?

REAGAN
I know we had such a meeting, but I don't recall what the outcome was or what we were discussing.

ATTORNEY
But you did have a meeting with Secretary Shultz and Secretary Weinberger and your other top advisers.

REAGAN
Yes.

ATTORNEY
What do you recall about it?

REAGAN
The Iranian representative suggested that we sell them a single shipment of TOW antitank missiles. And I made the decision that there was one thing upon which we could base selling the missiles, and that was that we had some nine hostages held by the Hezbollah, and that if they used their efforts to get our hostages freed, yes, we would make this sale. Some of our people said that this would—they didn't say it was trading for hostages, because it wasn't. My answer—they said it would be made to appear that way if it ever came to light. My answer to that was that if I had a child kidnapped and held for ransom, and I knew of someone who had perhaps the ability to get

that child back, it wouldn't be dealing with kidnappers to ask that individual to do that. And it would be perfectly fitting for me to reward that individual for doing that.

ATTORNEY
Do you recall making an analogy to the Lindbergh kidnapping?

REAGAN
I don't recall mentioning anyone else.

ATTORNEY
Do you recall Ed Meese having an opinion about involving Israel?

REAGAN
I don't recall that coming up at all, and as a matter of fact, to this day, I don't know who finished the delivery of the missiles.

ATTORNEY
Later you said at a press conference that the decision was yours and yours alone, and you referred to President Lincoln. Do you recall that?

REAGAN
No.

ATTORNEY
Do you recall having a conversation with Poindexter before Macfarlane went on his trip to Tehran?

REAGAN
I think I do. He brought in with him a Bible for me to autograph.

ATTORNEY
Do you recall Admiral Poindexter briefing you about Hawk missile parts being sent to Iran?

REAGAN
The only thing that I am aware of, and I cannot remember any meeting on this or not, was I do have a memory of learning or hearing that the Israelis, prior to these other things, had sent some of their Hawk missiles to Iran, evidently in that sale.

ATTORNEY
We were referring to a later shipment.

REAGAN
I just don't recall it.

ATTORNEY
Do you recall instructing Admiral Poindexter to put together a chronology of the Iran initiative?

REAGAN
No, I do not.

ATTORNEY
Do you recall having any discussion with Admiral Poindexter about reconstructing events?

REAGAN
I don't recall. I don't recall.

ATTORNEY
Did you and Admiral Poindexter brief administration officials or Congress about what had transpired?

REAGAN
I don't recall anything having to do with Congress in that sense.

ATTORNEY
Between your two addresses to the nation on November 13 and November 19, during which you discussed the initiative, did you receive information from Admiral Poindexter that helped you make those presentations?

REAGAN
I don't recall.

ATTORNEY
Would you have met with anyone?

REAGAN
I'm not denying whether I met with others. It's just that I don't recall.

ATTORNEY
Do you recall that at the end of the first press conference, Admiral Poindexter pointed out some information about Israel?

REAGAN
No, I don't. No.

ATTORNEY
On November 12, you met with congressional lead-

ers. Do you have any recollection of that meeting?

REAGAN
I know that someplace in there, there were meetings with the congressional leadership.

ATTORNEY
Was Admiral Poindexter present?

REAGAN
That I don't recall.

ATTORNEY
Did you tell the congressmen about the Hawk missile shipment that had taken place in November 1985?

REAGAN
No, I don't recall ever reporting that to anyone.

ATTORNEY
I'm told you were first informed of that shipment when you were in Geneva, preparing to meet with Mr. Gorbachev. Do you recall that?

REAGAN
I actually don't. I don't have any recollection about when I was told that or who told me. In a meeting of that kind over there in Geneva, there were so many meetings and so many places, and our great concern was that this was our first meeting with the general secretary, or secretary general, of the Soviet Union.

ATTORNEY
In other words—

REAGAN
What? I can't say that I specifically recall this meeting or that subject.

ATTORNEY
But at some point you became aware of the shipment?

REAGAN
That's right. As I say, I know that is in my memory, that I heard of France being connected with such a thing.

ATTORNEY
Ah, Mr. President—did you just say France?

REAGAN
I didn't think I did.

ATTORNEY
I'm sorry, I thought you said France.

REAGAN
If I did, it was a slip of the tongue.

ATTORNEY
When you met with the congressional leaders, you didn't recall the November 1985 shipment. Is that correct?

REAGAN

Let me just say I don't know when it would have been told to me or when I would have known.

ATTORNEY

But you heard about it before the report that appeared in that Lebanese newspaper.

REAGAN

No, I don't know. I can't say if it was before or after.

ATTORNEY

Did Admiral Poindexter tell you people in the White House had differing recollections of the November shipment?

REAGAN

No, I don't recall hearing that.

ATTORNEY

Do you recall asking Attorney General Meese if he could straighten things out?

REAGAN

No.

ATTORNEY

Do you recall Secretary Shultz telling you about the shipment in November of 1986?

REAGAN

I don't recall that.

ATTORNEY
When you testified before the Tower Commission, did you use notes?

REAGAN
I don't recall anything of that kind, because the Tower Commission was appointed by me.

ATTORNEY
Did you have trouble recollecting the shipment for the Tower Commission?

REAGAN
As I say, I only know that I, somewhere along the line, acquired that knowledge, and I don't know from whom or where.

ATTORNEY
Do you recall that the late Mr. Casey had to testify before Congress about that shipment?

REAGAN
I wasn't aware of that, no.

ATTORNEY
Do you recall talking to Poindexter about his meetings with members of the Senate and House Intelligence Committees?

REAGAN
No. But I have to point out that this continued saying "I don't recall" about so many of these meetings—I

have been told by statisticians that on the average I met with about eighty people a day for eight years, and I don't recall these meetings. And it's not because they weren't important, and I'm sure I dealt with things at the time, but I just—I just don't recall such a meeting.

ATTORNEY
But Congress was interested in this subject, wasn't it?

REAGAN
Oh, yes—they were fascinated.

"I Don't Want Any Criticism"

THERE USED TO BE A LOT OF SECRETS IN
America—presidents could have mistresses, journalists
would front for the CIA, the U.S. government would
run nuclear experiments on its citizens, and nobody
would ever hear about any of it. Perhaps the group
that had the most success in keeping its business private, however, was the Mafia. Of course, that was at a
time when fellows like Sam Giancana and Carlos Mar-
cello knew that J. Edgar Hoover, the director of the
FBI, liked to wear women's clothing. This may explain
why Hoover would insist there was no Cosa Nostra,
and then assign his agents to keep an eye on Leonard
Bernstein.

But for the last couple of decades, more highly moti-
vated law enforcement officials have gone after the
mob with gusto. Their favorite weapon has been the
wiretap, and thus we seem to know everything about
the mob. In fact, thanks to a bug that was planted in
the home of one of the leaders of the Patriarca crime
family of New England in 1989, we even know what
goes on during the most sacred and mysterious event in
a mafioso's life—the supersecret initiation rite.

The first men we meet are two important members
of the family—consigliere Joseph Russo and capo-

decime Vincent Ferrara. They're at the secret meeting place, a friend's home, a little before the secret ceremony is to begin.

JOSEPH RUSSO
Okay, we could put some seats over there, and some over there. Christ, these seats take up a lot of fuckin' space.

VINCENT FERRARA
You could put some there.

RUSSO
A lot of fuckin' space. And the food's gonna take up a lot of space. What are ya puttin' over there?

FERRARA
Ashtrays.

RUSSO
Fuck, Vinny, I told ya, this is a nonsmoking house. I don't want to see any ashtrays. If she smells smoke when she comes back, she's going to have a fit.

Two men enter, carrying steam trays.

RUSSO
Great, good, you got here. Put all that food in the kitchen. Put it on the table. And remember to put the striped cloth on! [*To Ferrara*] We're gonna need the other room.

FERRARA
Try this. [*Starts moving furniture.*] Make it like this,

and like this, and like this. We'll leave this chair here, and it'll be Raymond, you, me, and Charlie.

RUSSO
You could put Charlie there.

FERRARA
I don't want Charlie sitting there, because then people take it like he's over you, and he's not.

RUSSO
That's why the knights of the round table was round, so nobody was, ah, the boss.

FERRARA
Hey—they gotta know.

RUSSO
Of course. Tradition.

FERRARA
Tradition.

RUSSO
Protocol.

FERRARA
Protocol.

RUSSO
These guys don't hate me enough, now I'm in charge of this.

FERRARA
We gotta do the best we can, Joe.

RUSSO
I know.

FERRARA
And they're all stupid. What do you care what they think?

RUSSO
We just gotta do the best we can.

FERRARA
What I was going to think we should do is put the food on the coffee table.

RUSSO
Yeah, you're right. You're right, you're right, you're right. Now it looks like we're not all cluttered with food and shit. Now let's shut these blinds. How do I shut 'em?

FERRARA
You gotta shut 'em?

RUSSO
Look, I don't want any criticism from anybody in any way, shape, or form. It's best we shut them. If they want 'em open when they get here, we'll open 'em.

FERRARA
Okay, they're shut.

RUSSO
[*He starts to go down to the basement.*] Now I just want to do one more thing. Shut that door.

FERRARA
Shut this door?

RUSSO
Just talk a little louder when I'm down here.

FERRARA
What the fuck for?

RUSSO
What the fuck for? There's going to be guys down there, and I don't want them hearing what we say, that's what the fuck for, okay? Now talk out loud.

FERRARA
Okay. What should I say?

RUSSO
Whatever you want. [*Descends.*] Okay—

FERRARA
All right. Ladies and gentlemen, the star of the show, the new man in town, the captain, my main man, J.R. And on the way is the Donut Man. Can you hear me?

RUSSO
[*Reentering*] I did, but youse yellin' too loud.

FERRARA
You said talk out loud.

RUSSO
Yeah, but it was too loud. You go downstairs and I'll do it.

FERRARA
[*From downstairs*] Okay, go ahead.

RUSSO
All right, boys, we're going to do something for you today that just might make today the greatest day of your life. Did you hear that?

FERRARA
[*Returning*] I can hear your voice, but I can't distinguish the words.

RUSSO
Is there like a drone?

FERRARA
Yeah, a drone. What the fuck's the difference?

RUSSO
I just don't want any criticism or discussion.

Let's skip ahead to the actual inititation. Joe and Vinny are explaining things to the new man, Bobby. The don, Raymond Patriarca, is presiding.

RUSSO
Now, Bobby, as far as being introduced to another

"friend of ours," you never, never introduce yourself, under no conditions. The only way to meet another "friend of ours" is through another "friend."

FERRARA
You would never, never reveal that you are a made member unless properly introduced.

RUSSO
Never volunteer.

FERRARA
Never volunteer.

RUSSO
Another thing: we're very protective of our women. If you have a sister, unless our intentions are super-honorable—marriage, that would be all—we have nothin' to do with— Or if you have a girlfriend, or a wife, needless to say! Somethin' happens with somebody's wife, the only way you get outta that—

FERRARA
You die.

RUSSO
Yeah, you die. A woman is sacred.

FERRARA
It's different if your intentions are honorable.

RUSSO
Yeah! Like if a man has a sister, and you like his sis-

ter, and your intentions are honorable, and you want to get married and have a family and do the right thing, there's nothing wrong with that.

FERRARA
Nothin' at all.

RUSSO
In fact, we encourage intermarriage.

FERRARA
When your intentions are superhonorable.

RAYMOND PATRIARCA
[*Clears throat.*]

RUSSO
I believe the don now has a few words.

PATRIARCA
Bobby, you come here highly recommended. You done everything you hadda do, and everybody likes you. Here's what I have to say: stay the way youse are. Don't let bein' a member go to your head. Membership's not to be used to make money. It's not an advantage, or a ticket to abuse people. It doesn't make you better than other people. If you don't let it go to your head, and you don't abuse it, you'll have a happy, happy, happy life. Now teach him the Introduction.

RUSSO
[*Introducing Bobby to Vinny*] I say, "Say hello to a friend of ours, Bobby."

BOBBY
  Right.

RUSSO
  [*Continuing, reciprocating*] "Vinny, this is Bobby, a friend of ours."

BOBBY
  Right. Okay.

RUSSO
  Then you shake hands.

BOBBY
  Right.

RUSSO
  Don't kiss him. Years ago we used to kiss each other.

FERRARA
  We try to stop kissing in public.

RUSSO
  Yeah, now we try to stop it because—

FERRARA
  We stand out.

RUSSO
  Yeah, we stand out.

On the basis of this and twenty-three other wiretap-recording transcripts, Raymond, Joe, and Vinny were convicted of racketeering. And according to a newspaper report in October 1994, Joe and Vinny are still trying to manage the affairs of the Patriarca family, even though they're laboring under the disadvantage of imprisonment.

"It Was a Very Consensual Ménage à Trois"

IN THE SPRING OF 1992, THREE MEMBERS OF the New York Mets—Dwight Gooden, Daryl Boston, and Vince Coleman—were accused of raping a woman during the previous year's spring training. The accuser was a woman from New York who was a fan. Though authorities eventually decided not to prosecute, citing a lack of evidence, the police conducted a full investigation. Two of the interviews they held involved Mets who were not alleged to have been involved in the alleged rape. In the first, two detectives talk to David Cone, then a Met, now a Cy Young Award–winning pitcher for the Toronto Blue Jays, about some dates he had with the accuser, whom we'll call Sally.

DETECTIVE WILSON
How many times during spring training did you date Sally?

DAVID CONE
I would say approximately three times . . .

LIEUTENANT BARTAL
How far would you say that relationship went?

CONE
We had sex on all three dates, including the first time we met . . .

BARTAL
How long into the relationship were you, from the time you met her until it got intimate?

CONE
Within four hours.

BARTAL
When was the next time you were with Sally?

CONE
Within three or four days after that.

BARTAL
Now, the third time—

CONE
On the third occasion, the one girl, whose name you say is Lisa but whose name I don't recall, embarrassingly so—we were all together. For lack of a better cliché, it was a very consensual ménage à trois, in which they were both involved . . .

WILSON
Did any of the accused players discuss having sex with Sally?

CONE
Vince told me that Dwight and Daryl had sex with her, and that he didn't. That he, he maybe just was, uh, involved from an oral-sex nature.

BARTAL
Did that surprise you that Sally would have had sex with three blacks?

CONE
No. She seemed to me to be very modern in her thinking, very Manhattan, so to speak, if that makes sense. A very modern way of thinking. Nonprejudicial, in other words.

Two days later, Detective Wilson interviewed Sally's friend Lisa, also a big fan, who had accompanied her to Florida from New York. He asked her about a day that she and Sally spent with Cone and his fellow Met starter Ron Darling, whom they met one day at the ballpark after practice.

WILSON
Did they invite you to meet them for a drink?

LISA
Yeah. We went to David Cone's house. And one of their agents was over at the house for a while, too. It was Ron's agent, I think. His name was Steve. He was there for, like, the barbecue part, and the dinner, and the, um—while we watched a porn videotape.

WILSON
Did Steve participate in anything?

LISA
No.

WILSON
Did you guys kind of pair off?

LISA
I guess you could say that. Now we're getting to the embarrassing part.

WILSON
You tell me what happened first.

LISA
I was, like, really connecting with Dave there at the ballpark, right? If there was going to be any kind of pairing off, it was going to be, like, me and Dave, and Sally and whoever. And it turned out to be Ron. So before the four of us were hanging out, I was skinny-dipping and having sex with Dave in the swimming pool. And in the Jacuzzi. That was, like, my little seduction thing with my favorite baseball player. Then after we watched this porn video, I decided I wanted to be with Ron, too.

WILSON
Just kind of give me the scenario again.

LISA
I had fooled around with Dave in the swimming pool and the Jacuzzi, and I fooled around with Dave again while the others went out for beer. Then they came back, and we had dessert, and they put in this movie, and we're all hanging around, eating dessert, watching this movie, and Ron was making all this little comments like he was getting robbed by this movie. And,

and, and, um, so I was, like, well, you know, "This is my big chance!"

WILSON
   Sure.

LISA
   You know, I took it for what it was.

WILSON
   A one-day fantasy.

LISA
   Yeah! I mean, when we left that night, I was, like, screaming in the car, saying, "Pinch me, I know I'm dreaming!"

WILSON
   So you went with Ron—

LISA
   I mean, I felt like a total slut. By the time Ron and I were finished having sex, um, Dave and Sally were watching us, um, laughing, saying, "Hey! Encore! Encore!" Then by the time we got dressed, Ron pointed to the bedroom and said, "Check it out," and we watched them on the bed having sex.

To put the spring training experience in perspective, the accuser, "Sally," pointed out in her interview with the police that "My sex with Dave was incredibly normal, okay? Nothing out of the usual. Just very normal sex."

"You Still Think of Me as the Person You Married"

MOSTLY WE DON'T SEE THE REAL ENDS OF fairy tales—the vicious bickering between Jack and his mother after the golden goose dies; Hansel and Gretel's even crueler second stepmother; the part where the ugly duckling finds out that he's an ugly swan. But in the modern age, we have the Prince and Princess of Wales. Here they are at their country home in Highgrove, late one long night in 1992—the part of their tale where Charles and Diana are not living happily ever after.

PRINCE CHARLES
To be honest, I have never really thought about it.

PRINCESS DIANA
[*Bitterly*] Well, you wouldn't, would you?

CHARLES
Is there any reason why I should?

DIANA
Should what?

CHARLES
Think about.

DIANA
Do I have to?

CHARLES
Is this really getting us anywhere?

DIANA
Not particularly, no.

CHARLES
Shall I just go?

DIANA
I don't think that would solve anything.

CHARLES
It may allow us to get some sleep tonight.

DIANA
[*Loudly*] I couldn't sleep on this!

CHARLES
Look, three days is hardly a lifetime. Three days—

DIANA
My first reaction is, what do you mean by three days?

CHARLES
You know full well what I mean.

DIANA
Would you like to explain?

CHARLES
Circles, circles, round and round we go. I haven't seen anyone for days. God knows when I last picked up a newspaper or watched the TV. You make it sound as if this is all my fault personally. How can I explain something I don't even know?

DIANA
Well, there we are. Would you like to explain further?

CHARLES
Not now. Not here. Why?

DIANA
I want to know. I think it needs to be resolved.

CHARLES
But I keep saying, why here? Are you looking for a confrontation? Honestly, I don't want or need one. I just don't want or need one.

DIANA
But that's what we are getting to, because we are resolving nothing. Nothing is being decided. None of us will make a firm decision. A firm decision.

CHARLES
Is there really one needed now? We've spent all night going over the same thing without getting anywhere, and now you're making demands for a decision? Please be sensible.

DIANA

No, no, no, no, no. Let's decide it now, and then we can start afresh tomorrow morning. If nothing is decided now, we'll be in the same position tomorrow, next week, next month, as we are tonight. If there's just one godforsaken thing we can do, let's decide tonight.

CHARLES

I am trying to see things your way. I just can't. It's too late.

DIANA

Well, for once could you put yourself out and think of me?

CHARLES

[*Angrily*] Don't you dare to sit there and tell me to think of you. How the hell do you have the nerve to say that? I've done nothing but think of you and—

DIANA

No, no! don't believe that at all. For once, stop being so self-centered. You still think of me as the person you married.

CHARLES

I stopped thinking like that years ago.

DIANA

Yes, I suppose that would be a good indication of why we drifted apart, my dear.

CHARLES
Can I say anything right? Tell me what you want me to say.

DIANA
Say something I want to hear.

CHARLES
I'm leaving.

DIANA
Oh, don't be so bloody childish.

CHARLES
Oh, God.

DIANA
Must you always run when the pressure gets too much?

CHARLES
I'm not running. Unlike you, I want to deal with this like adults.

DIANA
I think I am. It's just that I want to get it done now rather than later. I don't want it to run on like a silly soap opera.

CHARLES
I'm going to bed.

DIANA

But why? You can sleep tomorrow. You can sleep anytime. But think of me for once—yes, think of me for once.

CHARLES

I'd rather think of the other parties involved. I don't know why, but right now I feel they are more important. You'll take care of that, you know that.

DIANA

How dare you be so presumptuous?

CHARLES

I'm tired. Good night.

DIANA

Look, you're doing it again! Come back. For Christ's sake, come back! How can you leave it like this?

CHARLES

I'll speak to you tomorrow.

DIANA

Oh, no, you won't.

CHARLES

Good night.

DIANA

Can you come in here, please?

"His Grandmother Is Always Looking At Me"

ON NEW YEAR'S EVE, 1989, EAVESDROPPERS
*from British intelligence taped the Princess of Wales
talking to her very close friend James Gilbey. It would
be nice to report that Gilbey was either a romantically
heroic person (duke, earl, knight errant, pretender to
the throne) or a romantically humble one (shepherd
boy, chimney sweep) or was otherwise distinguished
(poet, MP). Regrettably, he's a used-car salesman. The
way Diana and Gilbey kept in touch was that Gilbey
would go out in his car and drive around, and Di
would call him on his car phone. That way, they figured, no one could hear them talk.*

JAMES GILBEY
So, darling—what other lows today?

PRINCESS DIANA
That was it. I was very bad at lunch. I nearly started
blubbing. I felt really sad and empty, and I thought:
Bloody hell, after all I've done for this fucking family.

JAMES
You don't need to. 'Cause there are people out
there—and I've said this before—who will replace the
emptiness. With all sorts of things.

DIANA

I needn't ask horoscopes, but it is just so desperate. Always innuendo that I'm going to do something dramatic because I can't stand the confines of this marriage.

JAMES

I wouldn't worry about that. I think it's common knowledge, darling, amongst most people, that you don't have . . .

DIANA

A rapport?

JAMES

I think that comes through loud and clear. Darling, just forgetting that for a moment, how is Mara?

DIANA

She's all right. No, she's fine. She can't wait to get back.

JAMES

Can't she? When is she coming back?

DIANA

Saturday.

JAMES

Is she?

DIANA

Mmmmh.

JAMES
  I thought it was next Saturday.

DIANA
  No, Saturday.

JAMES
  Not quite as soon as you thought it was.

DIANA
  No.

JAMES
  Is she having a nice time?

DIANA
  Very nice.

JAMES
  Is she?

DIANA
  I think so. She's out of London. It gives her a bit of a
rest.

JAMES
  Yeah. Can't imagine what she does the whole
time.

DIANA
  No.

JAMES
   The restaurant. If you have a restaurant, it's so much
a part of your life, isn't it?

DIANA
   I know, people around you all the time.

JAMES
   That's right. The constant bossing and constant or-
dering and constant sort of fussing. And she hasn't got
that. She's probably been twiddling her fingers, wondering what to do.

DIANA
   Hmmmmmmm.

JAMES
   [*Snarkily*] Going to church every day . . .

DIANA
   I know.

JAMES
   Did you go to church today?

DIANA
   Yes, I did.

JAMES
   Did you, Squidge?

DIANA
   Yes.

JAMES
Did you say *lots* of prayers?

DIANA
Of course.

JAMES
Did you? Kiss me, darling. [*Sound of kisses being blown.*]

DIANA
[*Laughing, returns kiss.*]

JAMES
I can't tell you what a smile that has put on my face. I can't tell you. I was like a sort of caged rat, and Tony said, "You're in a terrible hurry to go." And I said, "Well, I've got things to do." Oh God. [*Sighs.*] I am not going to leave the phone in the car anymore, darling.

DIANA
No, please don't.

JAMES
No, I won't. And if it rings and someone says, "What on earth is your telephone ringing for?" I will say, "Oh, someone's got a wrong number or something."

DIANA
No, say one of your relations is not very well and your mother is just ringing in to give you progress.

JAMES

All right, so I will keep it near me, quite near to me tomorrow, because her father hates when I take the phone out shooting.

DIANA

Oh, you are out shooting tomorrow, are you?

JAMES

Yeah. And, darling, I will be back in London tomorrow night.

DIANA

Good.

JAMES

All right?

DIANA

Yes.

JAMES

Back on home territory, so no more awful breaks.

DIANA

No.

JAMES

Do you know, darling, I couldn't face the thought of not speaking to you. It fills me with real horror, you know.

DIANA
It's purely mutual.

JAMES
Is it? I really hate the idea of it, you know. It makes me really sort of scared.

• • •

JAMES
Darling—no sort of awful feelings of guilt, or—

DIANA
None at all.

JAMES
Remorse?

DIANA
None. None at all.

JAMES
Good.

DIANA
No, none at all. All's well.

JAMES
Okay, then, Squidgy. I am sorry you have had low times. Try, darling, when you get these urges—you just try to replace them with anger, like you did on Friday night, you know.

DIANA

I know. But do you know what's really quite—um—whatever the word is? His grandmother is always looking at me. With a strange look in her eyes. It's not hatred, it's sort of interest and pity mixed into one. I don't understand it. Every time I look up, she's looking at me. And then she looks away and smiles.

JAMES

Does she?

DIANA

Yes. I don't know what is going on.

JAMES

I should say to her one day, "I can't help but ask you. You are always looking at me. What is it? What are you thinking?" You must, darling. And interestingly enough, one of the things said to me today is that you are going to start standing up for yourself.

DIANA

Yes.

JAMES

We know that you are very capable of that, old Bossy Boots.

DIANA

I know, yes.

JAMES

What have you had on today? What have you been wearing?

DIANA
A pair of black jodhpur things on at the moment and a pink polo neck.

JAMES
Really. Looking good?

DIANA
Yes.

JAMES
Are you?

DIANA
Yes.

JAMES
Dead good?

DIANA
I think it's good.

JAMES
Do you?

DIANA
Yes.

JAMES
And what are on your feet?

DIANA
A pair of flat black pumps.

JAMES
Very chic.

DIANA
Yes.
[Pause in the tape.]
The redhead is being actually quite supportive.

JAMES
Is she?

DIANA
Yes, she has. I don't know why.

JAMES
Don't let the [*garbled*] down.

DIANA
No, I won't. I just talk to her about that side of things.

JAMES
You do? That's all I worry about. I just worry that, you know, she's sort of—she's desperately trying to get back in.

DIANA
She keeps telling me.

JAMES
She's trying to tag on to your [*garbled*]. She knows that your PR is so good. She's trying to tag on to that.

DIANA

Jimmy Savile rang me up yesterday and he said, "I'm just ringing up, my girl, to tell you that His Nibs has asked me to come and help out the redhead, and I'm just letting you know so that you don't find out through her or him. And I hope it's all right by you." And I said, "Jimmy, you do what you like."

JAMES

What do you mean, "help out the redhead," darling?

DIANA

With her publicity.

JAMES

Oh, has he?

DIANA

Sort her out. He said, "You can't change a lame duck, but I've got to talk to her, 'cause that's the boss's orders and I've got to carry them out. But I want to tell you that you're my number one girl, and I'm not—"

JAMES

Oh, darling, that's not fair. You're *my* number one girl.

DIANA

[*In the background*] Harry, it might be in my bathroom. [*Louder*] What did you say? *My bathroom!* [*To James*] What did you say? You didn't say anything about babies, did you?

JAMES
  No.

DIANA
  No?

JAMES
  Why, darling?

DIANA
  [*Laughing*] I thought you did.

JAMES
  Did you, darling? You have got them on the brain.

DIANA
  Well, yeah, maybe I—well, actually, I don't think I'm
going to be able to for ages.

JAMES
  I think you've got bored with the idea, actually.

DIANA
  I'm going to—

JAMES
  You are, aren't you? It was sort of a hot flush you
went through.

DIANA
  A very hot flush.

JAMES
Darling, when he says His Nibs rang him up, does he mean your other half or PA* rang him up?

DIANA
Eh? My other half.

JAMES
Your other half.

DIANA
Yes.

JAMES
Does he get on well with him?

DIANA
Sort of mentor. Talk in the mouthpiece—you moved away.

JAMES
Sorry, darling, I'm resting it on my chin. On my chinless. [*Sighs.*] Oh, I get so sort of possessive when I see all those pictures of you. I get so possessive. That's the least attractive aspect of me, really. I just see them and think: Oh, God, if only—

DIANA
There aren't that many pictures, are there? There haven't been that many.

---

*Prince Andrew, presumably.

JAMES
Four or five today.

DIANA
Oh.

JAMES
Various magazines. So, darling, I—

DIANA
I'm always smiling, aren't I?

JAMES
Always.

DIANA
I thought that today.

JAMES
I always told you that. It's what I call the old PR package, isn't it? As soon as you sense a camera—and I think you can sense a camera at a thousand yards—

DIANA
Yes.

JAMES
—that smile comes on, the charm comes out, and it stays there all the time, and then it goes away again.

• • •

JAMES
Darling, I wish we were going to be together tonight.

DIANA
I know. I want you to think of me after midnight. Are you staying up to see the New Year in?

JAMES
You don't need to encourage me to think about you. I have done nothing else for the last three months.

DIANA
Debbie says you are going to go through a transformation soon.

JAMES
I am?

DIANA
Yes. She says you are going to go through bits and pieces, and I've got to help you through them. Libra men, yeah. I said, "Great, I can do something back for him, he's done so much for me."

JAMES
Are you, Squidgy? Laugh some more—I love it when I hear you laughing. It makes me really happy when you laugh. Do you know I am happy when you're happy?

DIANA
I know you are.

JAMES
And I cry when you cry.

DIANA
I know. So sweet. The rate we are going, we won't need any dinner on Tuesday.

JAMES
No, I won't need any dinner, actually. Just seeing you will be all I need. I can't wait for Ken to ring. And I will be thinking of you after twelve o'clock. I don't need any reasons to even think about you. Mark Davis kept saying to me yesterday, "Of course, you haven't had a girlfriend for ages."

DIANA
Did you just get my hint about Tuesday night? I think you missed it. Think about what I said.

JAMES
No.

DIANA
I think you have missed it.

JAMES
No, you said, "At this rate, we won't want anything to eat."

DIANA
Yes.

JAMES
Yes, I know. I got there.

DIANA
Oh, well, you didn't exactly put the flag out.

JAMES
What, the surrender flag?

DIANA
Oh.

JAMES
Squidge, I was just going over it. I don't think I made too much reference to it.

DIANA
Oh, bugger.

JAMES
I don't think I made too much reference to it. Because the more you think about it, the more you worry about it.

DIANA
All right. I haven't been thinking a lot else.

JAMES
Haven't you?

DIANA
  No.

JAMES
  Well, I can tell you, that makes two. You know, all I want to do is get in my car and drive around the country, talking to you.

DIANA
  Thanks. [*Laughter*]

JAMES
  That's all I want to do, darling. I just want to see you and be with you. That's what's going to be such bliss, being back in London.

DIANA
  I know.

JAMES
  I mean, it can't be a regular future, darling, I understand that, but it would be nice if you are at least next door.

DIANA
  Yes.

JAMES
  What's that noise?

DIANA
  The television. Drowning my conversation.

JAMES
Can you turn it down?

DIANA
No.

JAMES
Why?

DIANA
Because it's covering my conversation.

JAMES
All right. I got Tuesday night, don't worry. I got there. I can tell you, the feeling's entirely mutual. Ummmmmm, Squidgy—what else? It's like unwinding now. I am just letting my heartbeat come down again now. I had the most amazing dream about us last night. Not physical.

DIANA
That makes a change.

JAMES
Darling, it's just that we were together an awful lot of the time, and we were having dinner with some people. It was the most extraordinary dream, because I woke up in the morning and I remembered all aspects of it—what you were wearing, and what you had said. It was so strange—very strange, and very lovely, too. Oh, Squidgy, kiss me! [*Sound of both of them kissing*] Oh, God, it's wonderful, isn't it? This sort of feeling? Don't you like it?

DIANA
I love it. I love it.

JAMES
Isn't it absolutely wonderful? I haven't had it for years. I feel about twenty-one again.

DIANA
Well, you're not, you're thirty-three.

JAMES
I know.

•   •   •

JAMES
Oh, to go back to another point—about your mother-in-law, no, your grandmother-in-law. I think the next time, you just want to outstare her, and that's easy.

DIANA
No, no, listen. It's affection. Affection. It's definitely affection. It's sort of—it's not hostile, anyway.

JAMES
Oh, isn't it?

DIANA
No. She's sort of fascinated by me but doesn't know how to unravel it.

JAMES
I'm sorry, darling. I thought you meant hostile.

DIANA
Did you see *News of the World?*

JAMES
No, but you should read *The People,* darling.
There's a very good picture of you.

DIANA
Arrr.

JAMES
Oh, no, it's—where is there a good picture? In the
Express, was there? I think there's a—wearing that
pink, very smart pink top. That excellent pink top.

DIANA
Oh, I know, I know.

JAMES
Do you know the one that I mean?

DIANA
I know.

JAMES
Very good. Shit hot, actually.

DIANA
Shit hot. [*Laughs*]

JAMES
Shit hot.

DIANA
Fergie said to me today that she had lunch with Nigel Havers and all he could talk about was me. And I said, "Oh, Fergie, how awful for you." And she said, "Don't worry, it's the admiration club." A lot of people talk to her about me, which she can't help.

JAMES
I tell you, darling, she is desperate to tag on to your coattails.

DIANA
Well, she can't.

JAMES
No, she absolutely can't. Now you have to make that quite clear.

DIANA
If you want to be like me, you have to suffer.

JAMES
Oh, Squidgy!

DIANA
Yeah. You have to. And then you get what you—

JAMES
Get what you want.

DIANA
No. Get what you deserve, perhaps.

JAMES
Yes, such as a secondhand-car dealer.

DIANA
Yes, I know.

• • •

JAMES
Oh, Squidgy, I love you, love you, love you.

DIANA
You are the nicest person in the world.

JAMES
Pardon?

DIANA
The nicest person in the world.

JAMES
Well, darling, you are to me, too. Sometimes.

DIANA
What do you mean, sometimes?

• • •

DIANA
Oh, James, darling, you're driving me *crazy!* I'm getting so hot and horny! Oh, James, if you don't stop, I'm going to climax!

JAMES
[*Moaning*] Squidgy, kiss me! You don't mind it, darling, when I talk to you so much?

DIANA
Oh, no, I love it. Never *had* it before.

•   •   •

JAMES
Darling, how are the boys?

DIANA
Very well.

JAMES
Are they having a good time?

DIANA
Yes, very happy. Seem to be.

JAMES
That's nice. Have you been looking after them today?

DIANA
Well, I've been with them a lot, yes.

JAMES
Has he been looking after them?

DIANA
Oh, no, not really. My God, you know!

JAMES

Have you seen him at all today, apart from lunch?

DIANA

I have. We went out to tea. It's just so difficult, so complicated. He makes my life real, real torture, I've decided.

JAMES

Tell me more.

DIANA

But the distancing will be because I go out and—I hate the word—I conquer the world. I don't mean that, I mean I'll go out and do my bit in the way I know how and I leave him behind. That's what I see happening.

JAMES

Did you talk in the car?

DIANA

Yes, but nothing in particular. He said he didn't want to go out tonight.

JAMES

Did you have the kids with you?

DIANA

No.

JAMES

What, you went by yourselves?

DIANA
No, they were behind us.

JAMES
Oh, were they? How did he enjoy it?

DIANA
I don't know. He didn't really comment.

JAMES
No. Oh, Squidgy. Kiss me, please.
The sound of kisses.

At one point in the conversation, Diana analyzes James's wardrobe. After she criticizes his brown suede Guccis:

"I will give you some money. You can go off and spend it for me."

"I'm a connoisseur in that department," she says.

"Well, you think you are," he says.

"Well, I've decked out people in my time."

"Who did you deck out? Not too many, I hope."

"James Hewitt," she replies, speaking the name of the man who will later write a kiss-and-tell book about their relationship and with whom she was photographed by the British Secret Service in the act of intercourse. "Entirely dressed him from head to foot, that man. Cost me quite a bit."

"What, he didn't even pay you to do it?"

"No."

"God. Very extravagant, darling."

"Well," she replies, "I am, aren't I?"

"A Pair of Knickers"

WE WERE SHOCKED—SHOCKED—TO DIS-
*cover that the marriage of Charles, the Prince of Wales,
and Diana, the Princess of Wales, is an empty and
loveless arrangement that would have been over a long
time ago if they were mere humans. We were also
shocked—and, all right, excited—to discover that the
British Secret Service routinely spies on the royal family, eavesdropping on their telephone conversations
and videotaping their assignations, at least ones involving Diana and memoir-writing equestrian friends. Yet
we have as a result been treated to some telling conversations that teach us a lot about royal life—its exquisite
Pinteresque tedium, for instance, and the fact that the
plumbing in the royal residences isn't up to modern
standards.*

*Anyway, here's the scene: It's late at night, a week
before Christmas 1989 (just days before James Gilbey
called Diana "Squidgy"). Charles is on the phone in
Cheshire, in the north of England. His extremely good
friend Camilla Parker Bowles is speaking from Wilt-
shire in the south.*

PRINCE CHARLES
He was a bit anxious, actually.

CAMILLA PARKER BOWLES
Was he?

CHARLES
He thought he might have gone a bit far.

CAMILLA
Aw, well.

CHARLES
Anyway, you know, that's the sort of thing one has to be aware of. And sort of feel one's way along with, if you know what I mean.

CAMILLA
Mmmm. You're awfully good at feeling your way along.

CHARLES
Oh, stop! I want to feel my way along you, all over you and up and down you.

CAMILLA
Oh, that's just what I need at this moment.

CHARLES
Is it?

CAMILLA
I know it would revive me. I can't bear a Sunday night without you. I can't start the week without you.

CHARLES
I fill up your tank!

CAMILLA
Yes, you do!

CHARLES
Then you can cope.

CAMILLA
Then I'm all right.

CHARLES
What about me? The trouble is, I need you several times a week.

CAMILLA
Mmmm. So do I. I need you all week, all the time.

CHARLES
Oh, God, I'll just live inside your trousers or something. It would be much easier!

CAMILLA
What are you going to turn into, a pair of knickers? Oh, you're going to come back as a pair of knickers.

CHARLES
Or, God forbid, a Tampax, just my luck.

CAMILLA
You are a complete idiot! Oh, what a wonderful idea.

CHARLES
My luck to be chucked down a lavatory and go on

and on forever, swirling round on the top, never going down.

CAMILLA
Oh, darling!

CHARLES
Until the next one comes through.

CAMILLA
Or perhaps you could just come back as a box.

CHARLES
What sort of box?

CAMILLA
A box of Tampax, so you could just keep going.

CHARLES
That's true.

CAMILLA
Repeating yourself. Oh, darling. Oh, I just want you now.

CHARLES
Do you?

CAMILLA
Mmmm.

CHARLES
So do I.

CAMILLA
   Desperately; desperately; desperately . . . Gone to sleep?

CHARLES
   No, I'm here.

CAMILLA
   You see, the problem is, I've got to be in London to-morrow night.

CHARLES
   Yes.

CAMILLA
   And Tuesday night, A's* coming home.

CHARLES
   No.

CAMILLA
   Would you believe it? Because I don't know what he's doing, he's shooting down here or something. But, darling, you wouldn't be able to ring me anyway, would you?

CHARLES
   I might just. I mean, tomorrow night I could have done.

------

   *"A" is her husband of twenty years, Andrew, from whom she filed for divorce in 1995.

CAMILLA
   Oh, darling, I can't bear it. How could you have done tomorrow night?

CHARLES
   Because I'll be [*yawns*] working on the next speech.

CAMILLA
   Oh, no; what's the next one?

CHARLES
   A Business in Communities one, rebuilding communities.

CAMILLA
   Oh, no, when's that for?

CHARLES
   A rather important one for Wednesday.

CAMILLA
   Well, at least I'll be behind you. [*Pause*] Darling—

CHARLES
   But oh, God, when am I going to speak to you?

CAMILLA
   I can't bear it.

CHARLES
   Wednesday night?

CAMILLA
   Oh, certainly Wednesday night. I'll be alone, um,

Wednesday, you know, the evening. And early Wednesday morning. I mean, he'll be leaving half past eight, quarter past eight. He won't be here Thursday, pray God. Oh, darling, I think I'll—

CHARLES
Pray. Just pray.

CAMILLA
It would be so wonderful to have just one night to set us on our way, wouldn't it?

CHARLES
Wouldn't it? To wish you a happy Christmas?

CAMILLA
Oh, let's don't think about Christmas. I can't bear it. [*Pause*] Gone to sleep? I think you'd better, don't you, darling?

CHARLES
Yes, darling.

CAMILLA
I think you've exhausted yourself by all that hard work. You must go to sleep now. Darling?

CHARLES
Yes, darling?

CAMILLA
Will you ring me when you wake up?

CHARLES
Yes, I will.

CAMILLA
Night night, my darling.

CHARLES
Darling.

CAMILLA
I do love you.

CHARLES
Try and ring.

CAMILLA
Yeah, if I can. Love you, darling.

CHARLES
Night, darling.

CAMILLA
I do love you.

CHARLES
Love you, too. Don't want to say good-bye.

CAMILLA
Well done for doing that. You're a clever old thing. An awfully good brain lurking there, isn't there? Oh, darling, I think you ought to give the brain a rest now. Night night.

CHARLES
  Night, darling. God bless.

CAMILLA
  I do love you, and I'm so proud of you.

CHARLES
  Oh, I'm so proud of you.

CAMILLA
  Don't be silly. I've never achieved anything.

CHARLES
  Yes, you have.

CAMILLA
  No, I haven't.

CHARLES
  Your great achievement is to love me.

CAMILLA
  Oh, darling. Easier than falling off a chair.

CHARLES
  You suffer all these indignities and tortures and calumnies.

CAMILLA
  Oh, darling, don't be silly. That's love. It's the strength of love. Night night.

CHARLES
  Night, darling. Sounds as though you're dragging an enormous piece of string behind you with hundreds of tin pots and cans attached to it. I think it must be your telephone. [*Blows kiss.*] Night.

CAMILLA
  Love you.

CHARLES
  Don't want to say good-bye.

CAMILLA
  Neither do I, but you must get some sleep. Bye.

CHARLES
  Bye, darling.

CAMILLA
  Love you.

CHARLES
  Bye.

CAMILLA
  Hopefully talk to you in the morning.

CHARLES
  Please.

CAMILLA
  Bye. I do love you.

CHARLES
Night.

CAMILLA
Night.

CHARLES
Night.

CAMILLA
Bye-bye.

CHARLES
Going.

CAMILLA
Bye.

CHARLES
Going.

CAMILLA
Gone.

CHARLES
Night.

CAMILLA
Bye. Press the button.

CHARLES
Going to press the tit.

CAMILLA
  All right, darling. I wish you were pressing mine.

CHARLES
  God, I wish I was! Harder and harder!

CAMILLA
  Oh, darling!

CHARLES
  Night.

CAMILLA
  Night.

CHARLES
  Love you.

CAMILLA
  [*Yawning*] Love you. Press the tit.

CHARLES
  Adore you. Night.

CAMILLA
  Night.

CHARLES
  Night.

CAMILLA
  [*Blows a kiss.*]

CHARLES
Night.

CAMILLA
Good night, my darling. Love you.